GOD, I'M WORRIED ABOUT MY SON

GOD, I'M WORRIED ABOUT MY SON

The Christian Mom's Guide
to Finding Common Ground
with a Rebellious Teen

VAL MITCHELL

ISBN: 9798864667644

Dedication

To my beloved family and friends,
And to the extraordinary leaders who guided me.
This book would not have been possible without you.

Contents

A Special Gift for You

Congratulations! You are now on your way to discovering how to reach a common ground with your son. I'm excited about your journey ahead. I pray that as you read each chapter, God meets you.

In return for making this incredible decision, I want to offer you another resource I created. In return for making this incredible decision, I want to offer you a free, insightful video. Discover invaluable tools and techniques to foster understanding and find common ground with your rebellious teenage son. This gift, valued at $97, is yours for free. It's my way of saying thank you for choosing to find common ground.

For your free copy, visit:

Gift.WorriedAboutMySon.com

You can also find me LIVE on Facebook – *Praying in My Car*. Here, I share biblical principles and teachings that empower and refuel the soul. Connect with me by joining the group. www.Facebook.com/OK2Pray

Thank you again for allowing me to share how I rediscovered a relationship with my rebellious teenage son.

Introduction

Introduction

"Being a mother is learning about strengths
you didn't know you had
and dealing with fears you didn't know existed."
Nishan Panwar

How many nights have you spent struggling to save a child who doesn't want to be saved? I've been there. Countless nights of lying awake, worried over his whereabouts and the people he associated with. His unpredictable moods, intense emotions, and impulsive actions taxed me mentally and physically.

Motherhood is an incredible gift but comes with its fair share of challenges, especially when raising a rebellious teenage son. For numerous nights, I grappled with rescuing a child who refused to be saved.

Having big plans for his life, I enrolled him in the right schools because college was the end goal. I even supported his involvement in sports and music. I monitored his social media usage and kept track of his friends. Every Sunday, we attended church and participated in teenage ministry. I thought these activities would instill values and keep him on the right path, but despite trying these methods, none worked. As a result, he decided to take a different approach.

He started becoming more secretive. This included skipping school and hanging out with friends I didn't care for. His unpredictable moods, intense emotions, and impulsive actions tax me mentally and physically. Countless nights, I lay awake, worried over his whereabouts and the people he associated with.

I masked the shame because I was tired of hearing advice from those whose sons lived my desired lifestyle. I could no longer watch helplessly as various aspects of his life fell away, but as much as I wanted to give up, something within wouldn't allow me to lose hope.

Frantically, I searched for a guidebook containing any necessary steps to navigate his and my trials. My search yielded nothing, which intensified my frustration the more.

Let's face it: motherhood is undoubtedly a painstaking responsibility. Dealing with a teenager's disobedience is exhausting. Life felt out of control.

If you can relate to this, then we share something in common. We are concerned for our sons because witnessing their struggles has become incredibly challenging. I can feel the desperation and love in your heart as you yearn to rescue him but fail at every attempt.

I've been in your shoes. Shed the same tears and beat me up with the same guilt. As a career mom, I focused on everyday must-dos that I no longer recognized him when he transitioned into his teenage years. He hated everything he once loved. Including me - and didn't mind telling me either.

FACTS AND STATISTICS

I worried my son would become a statistic. Did you know that research states that teenagers with rebellious behavior also have thoughts of suicide? I learned that suicide is the second-leading cause of death among people aged 15 to 24 in the U.S. For young African American males,[1] the suicide rate from 2018-2022 increased by 20%.[2]

Nearly 20% of high school students report having thoughts of suicide, and 9% have attempted to take their lives.[3]

"Teenagers and young adults have had rising rates of suicide compared to 10 or 15 years ago," says Carl Fleisher, MD, who specialized in adolescent and child psychiatry at UCLA Health and is now at Boston Child Study Center in Los Angeles.

Harry Miller, an Ohio State football player, shares his revelations on his attempted suicide. In a Twitter post, he states, "This is not an issue reserved for the far and away," wrote Miller. "It is in our homes. It is in our conversations. It is in the people we love."[4]

There is a blurred line between a rebellious teen and one on the brink of suicide. Sometimes, distinguishing between a phase and a serious threat can be difficult. I found out the hard way that my son landed in this category. I had no idea he contemplated whether to live or die.

YOU ARE NOT ALONE

I consider that our present sufferings are not worth comparing with the glory that will be revealed in us.
Romans 8:18 (NIV)

God has come to restore order, heal your troubled mind, and restore peace for you and your son.

I challenge you today. Don't give up on your son. As a Christian mother, with God, you can uplift your son's self-esteem.

Our sons deserve to flourish and overcome their challenges. Low self-esteem is robbing them of their well-being, relationships, and future success.

God asked me to share my story.

Before writing this book, I decided to understand what worries kept other mothers up at night. Through these conversations, I discovered that mothers faced many anxieties regarding their sons' emotional well-being. The most distressing aspect was seeing their sons waver between good days and bouts with rebellious behavior.

Communication barriers were also a significant source of concern. They found it challenging to express their emotions and thoughts openly without their sons feeling attacked. Lastly, some mothers expressed unease over their sons' behavior. They witnessed their sons' self-destructive actions, such as substance abuse, self-harm, or delinquent activities, which caused them great worry and distress.

As I delved into their stories, my heart stirred with mixed emotions. I was surprised by our similarities in dealing with our son's challenging behavior. I remember the challenges and complexities we often face - uncertainty, strained relationships, and moments of desperation. The depth of our struggles, the weight of our responsibilities, and the joys that come with the privilege of being a mother.

God confirmed then the need for me to share my story.

WHAT'S MY APPROACH?

Let's have an honest conversation about your son's struggles, and together, we'll explore practical and biblical steps to build up his self-worth.

I am a mother who chose to do whatever I could to help my son. God gave me the tools to guide me toward realigning my son with His plans. God desires to do the same for your son.

I hear you, "Why should I listen to you?"

I am a devoted mother determined to equip other mothers with the same tools God gave me to help my son rise above self-doubt and embrace his true potential.

In a world that often magnifies insecurities, I experienced first-hand how God's assistance helped my son overcome his.

We will explore the factors that influence their self-perception, the role of a mother in shaping their confidence, and practical strategies to instill a profound sense of self-assuredness. Drawing from expert and biblical insights and real-life experiences, this guide offers invaluable wisdom to help mothers inspire their teenage sons to flourish as confident, capable, and compassionate individuals.

I've divided these powerful biblical self-managing tools God taught me into three distinct sections: *"The Discovery,"* *"Attaining Understanding,"* and *"Practical Solutions."* These are guaranteed to increase your effectiveness in leading your son toward self-acceptance, confidence, and a renewed belief in his worth.

The Discovery

In this section, we embark on a journey into the lives of two teenage sons raised in different households as they face their struggles with defiance. Through their challenges, their mothers cry out to God for help. By examining their experiences, we can gain insights into our journeys as mothers of teenage sons and learn from the family's mistakes.

Section Focus Topics

- The Story of My Son
- The Story of Hagar's Son Ishmael

Attaining Understanding

Moving forward, we delve deeper into the underlying reasons behind our teenage sons' rebellious tendencies. We will break down their mindsets, including the contributing factors, to identify the root of their rebellion.

Section Focus Topics

- An Adolescent Mindset
- A Healthy Mindset

Practical Solutions

This last section presents a comprehensive array of reliable resources and God-given practical strategies. Additionally, I share a personal account of how these solutions, rooted in faith, played a pivotal role in reuniting my family, highlighting the transformative power of faith-based approaches.

Section Focus Topics

- Nurturing A Healthy Self-Esteem
- Cultivating a Supportive Environment
- Increasing in the Fruit of the Spirit
- Facing the Man in the Mirror
- Understanding the Five Love Languages
- Opening Lines of Communication
- Building Unity

Let's Get Started

Together, let us embark on this empowering voyage as we uncover the secrets to building the firm foundation of self-esteem that our sons need to thrive in a complex world.

After finishing each chapter, you will have opportunities to pray alongside a guided prayer, read scriptures and affirmations, and apply practical applications your son can join in with you.

By the end of this book, you will know how to unlock his inner strength through a powerful intersection of faith and trust in God's plan for his life.

Here is a checklist of what you'll need before getting started.

A Journal

Maintain a journal to jot down your thoughts, prayers, and reflections. This can be a tangible reminder of God's presence with you during this journey. Furthermore, it will aid in recalling all the necessary action steps. It is a reliable reference when revisiting a previously learned lesson.

An Encouragement Board

Create an encouragement board or space to pin the scriptures, affirmations, and inspiring quotes collected throughout the book. Use them as a visual reminder of your faith and hope.

Prayer Partner(s)

Grab a prayer partner with whom you can agree about saving your son. Share with them your specific prayer requests. This practice can deepen your connection to God and offer mutual support.

After each chapter, I include a guided prayer to invite you to take your learning to God for more revelation. I encourage you to use the one shown or personalize it to better reflect your thoughts and feelings. The prayer is meant to set aside time to connect with God.

A Bible

It is essential to be open to God's guidance. The Bible can bring clarity to what God is speaking at that moment. It is also a great resource to gain more insight and understanding of the referenced scriptures and biblical characters you'll learn about throughout this reading.

Commitment to Implement

To win back your son effectively, I need your commitment to setting aside time to implement what you learned. Don't worry. I will share practical steps you can take.

There is hope for brighter days. I've been where you are. We share the same desire. I was worried about my son, and God kept His promise. He helped my son. That same God will also be there for your son, too. Allow this guide to help you find common ground with your rebellious son.

CHAPTER 1

In It for the
Long Haul

*"Most of the important things in the world have been
accomplished by people who have kept on trying when there
seemed to be no hope at all."*
Dale Carnegie

A s Christians, we share a belief that Jesus is good. This belief has us attend church on Sundays, listen to weekly devotionals, and participate in corporate prayer.

When I was young, my mother took me to church, and that's how I learned about God. I loved listening to the choir sing and watching the pastor give his sermon. However, once Monday came around, I returned to my routine and didn't think much about God until the following Sunday.

I thought because I attended church, it made me a good Christian. I never realized that neglecting God throughout the rest of the week caused me to lose what mattered most—my son.

He fell into a dark place of hopelessness and despair, and I could not pull him out.

When God stepped in, winning back my son did not happen overnight. There were days when I wondered if God had forgotten His commitment. Though the process wasn't easy, I continued to fast and pray.

Success never arrives overnight. Doing things well takes time and effort like a grandmother preparing her famous banana nut bread. She understands the value of patience. Before it's served on Sunday morning, she always follows a specific baking process.

First, she pulls out the past-down recipe. Next, she prepares the ingredients:

> *Very ripe bananas*
> Melted butter
> Baking soda
> Pinch salt
> Sugar
> Egg
> Vanilla extract
> All-purpose flour
> *Greased loaf pan*

She preheats the oven, mixes the ingredients, and pours the mixture into a loaf pan.

After patience and time, that delicious comfort food we have been waiting for is available for everyone to enjoy.

For Grandma's famous bread, her two most important ingredients are the ripe bananas and the loaf pan.

As we walk this journey, our two most essential ingredients are your son (ripe bananas) and God (loaf pan). Our job is to gather all the ingredients (the tools you'll learn from this book and your son) and pour them into God (the loaf pan). He will take (placing in the oven) and release him once He and your son are ready.

Always keep this in mind. Trust God. Trust the Process. Success is a process. It takes time and effort to do things well.

Allow me to caution you in advance. Walking through this journey, you will encounter some obstacles. Mine was my son considering suicide. *Thank You God, for Intervening! He stopped my son's plans to take his life.*

Now that you asked God to intervene, things with your son might take a turn for the worse. In those moments, it's natural to feel disheartened. But I urge you not to lose sight of the bigger picture and the promise God holds for your son's future. God has a way of beginning with the end in mind. And sometimes, the path to that better outcome can be rough before it smoothens.

Remember the story of Egypt and how Mose arrived to liberate the Israelites who cried out to God for their release from slavery? They had to endure significant torment from the Egyptians before gaining their freedom. Despite the hardships they faced, they persevered and ultimately prevailed.

Concentrating solely on the beginning of God's intervention will overlook the broader perspective - the fulfillment of God's commitment after He promised to help. Had the Israelites departed Egypt as soon as Moses arrived, they would have foregone the opportunity to leave with the Egyptians' treasures.

Initially, the Israelites and my son's circumstances did get more brutal, but it was all part of God's plan for them to receive their full reward.

Yes, starting down this path will become uneasy before it gets better.

- After I cried out to God, I learned my son planned to take his life.
- After the Israelites cried out for help, God hardened Pharaoh's heart, leading him to increase their torment.

Don't focus on the beginning. Keep the end goal in mind and believe God will remain faithful to his promise, and eventually, everyone emerges more robust and better off.

- My relationship with my son strengthened as he has gained a new perspective on life.
- Freedom came to the Israelites with the bonus of leaving with the Egyptians' treasures.

When the challenging moments arrive, lean on God to help with the navigation. Keep praying, keep believing, and hold on to that unwavering hope that you will reach common ground. Your prayers are making a difference, and God is working, even if it's not immediately apparent.

· · ·

Now that you're ready to resume the race, let's invite Jesus to join us on the journey.

Hebrews 12:2 tells us Jesus is the champion who initiates and strengthens our faith. Throughout this journey, I urge you to persevere until the end. Let Christ complete the work. If you always focus steadfastly on Him, He will run alongside you.

> *Trust in the Lord with all your heart and lean not on your understanding; in all your ways submit to him, and he will make your paths straight.*
> —Proverbs 3:5-6

During uncertain times, I find comfort in this verse. It encourages me to rely on God's wisdom and understanding instead of my limited perspective. I encourage you to surrender your initial plans and seek God's guidance. Trust in His wisdom to help you and your son navigate this process.

Now, let's invite God into the journey. While reading this prayer, believe that God hears you, sees you, and knows how to get you through.

THOUGHTS TO PONDER

Prayer

Pray this prayer aloud.

"Heavenly Father,

I seek Your guidance and support as I face challenges alongside my son. You are the source of all wisdom and understanding, and I ask for Your wisdom to help me comprehend and navigate the complexities of his struggles.

Lord, I ask for Your divine intervention and healing in my son's life. Touch him with Your peace, strength, and comfort. Surround him with supportive friends, mentors, and resources to aid him on his journey to wholeness and a renewed mindset. I trust in Your perfect timing and Your plan for his life.

I surrender my concerns and fears into Your loving hands, knowing that You are with us every step of the way. Strengthen my faith, Lord, and help me to trust in Your unfailing love continually.

In Jesus' name. Amen."

May your faith in God's plan for your son's life be a source of strength and encouragement, guiding you through this journey of motherhood with love and hope.

Remember, you are not alone. Our loving and caring God hears your prayers. Trust the process and continue to support your son with love.

Here are some scriptures and affirmations to bolster your faith and trust. Allow God's Word to minister to you, your faith, and your trust in Him. Read them aloud every day, then write them down. Using your encouragement board, post them where you will see them often.

Scriptures

- "And without faith it is impossible to please him, for whoever would draw near to God must believe that he exists and that he rewards those who seek him." (Hebrews 11:6)
- "Trust in the Lord with all your heart, and do not lean on your own understanding. In all your ways acknowledge him, and he will make straight your paths." (Proverbs 3:5-6)
- "Commit your way to the Lord; trust in him, and he will act. He will bring forth your righteousness as the light, and your justice as the noonday." (Psalm 37:5-6)

Reciting affirmations out loud can provide numerous positive outcomes. I selected affirmations that would serve as a gentle nudge toward achieving your goal of finding common ground. As you read them, engage both your words and senses. This will help the affirmations become even more memorable.

Think of it as painting a vivid picture of positivity in your mind. Every affirmation listed has the power to reshape your thoughts about yourself, reminding you of the incredible inner strength you possess. I recommend reading them often and adding those that speak to you directly to your encouragement board.

Affirmations

- "I am worthy of God's love and grace, and I trust in His divine plan for my life and my son's journey."
- "I release all fears and doubts, knowing that God's presence surrounds me, guiding and uplifting me in every situation."
- "Each day, my faith grows stronger, and I find peace, joy, and strength in embracing my spirituality."

Practical Application

1. Write in your journal the lesson you learned from this chapter.
2. Establish a time to pray daily for thirty minutes without interruption.
3. Commit to reading the above scriptures and affirmations at least once per day to help strengthen you as you prepare for the journey ahead.

Text your son this affirmation today.

"You are a unique and valuable individual, worthy of love, respect, and all the goodness life offers."

Let's save your son!

Section One

DISCOVERY

The Discovery Section

"The Lord is good, a stronghold in the day of trouble;
He knows those who take refuge in him."
Nahum 1:7 ESV

WHAT YOU WILL DISCOVER

In "The Discovery" section, you begin the journey by discovering others who share your story. First, you will learn about my experiences walking in your shoes with my teenage son. You will see why I can relate to the exhaustion of endless arguments and disagreements.

Next, I share the Biblical story about a teenage boy named Ishmael. He faced turmoil in his home, which caused him to become a rebellious adult. Ishmael was the son of Hagar and Abraham, and he couldn't escape the emotional imprints from his youth. As the Bible describes, he became "a wild donkey of a man."

You will learn about two boys who grew up in different environments but ended up with rebellious behavior. By standing up for our sons now, with the help of God, we can change the trajectory of their future.

The Goodness of The Lord

John 6:37 tells us Jesus will never reject anyone who comes to Him. When we encounter trouble, God's love welcomes us back, even if we initially try to solve the problem ourselves.

When it seems God closed the doorway because of unanswered prayers, He is faithful to leave a window open. God wants us to dwell in His love, so He always has an open path.

Imagine a house with a shut front door. His will isn't for us to remain outside, so He provides another way– the open window. However, before entering, we must lower our posture before we can fit through.

> *"If my people, who are called by my name, will humble themselves and pray and seek my face and turn from their wicked ways, then I will hear from heaven, and I will forgive their sin and will heal their land."*
> —2 Chronicles 7:14

This verse is that open window to enter His presence. Notice how it calls out Humility. That's how you can fit through the open window.

To Humble = Not proud or arrogant. Having a spirit of submission or deference.

24

Once inside, there are still some things He requires of us.

Pray – Speak to him directly.

Seek His Face – Keep calling out to Him until He answers, believing you will find him.

Turn from Your Wicked Ways – Repent. Apologize for all your wrongdoings, including not including Him in raising your son.

This step of repentance is crucial. We must remove all obstacles of sin before seeking God's intervention. Repentance allows God to forgive and cleanse us of sins. Psalm 84:11 says, "If I had not confessed the sin in my heart, the Lord would not have listened."

Before entering "The Discovery" section, it is essential to take the following steps: humble yourself, seek God's face through prayer, and turn away from any wicked ways. By doing so, God promises to forgive, hear from heaven, and heal.

Together, let's work towards healing our sons.

CHAPTER 2

My Son's Story

My Gift from The Lord

> *"Children are a gift from the Lord;*
> *they are a reward from him."*
> Psalm 127:3 NLT

Sixteen years later, I vividly recall the moment I first held my son. Looking into his tiny brown eyes, joy overflowed. Tears streamed down my cheeks as we embraced. In that remarkable moment, all worries and uncertainties dissipated, replaced by an overwhelming sense of awe and wonder. Every feature, every delicate detail of this precious child, seemed like a miracle before my eyes.

I marveled at this incredible gift bestowed upon me. Overwhelmed by a profound sense of gratitude, I whispered a prayer of thanks to the heavens, cherishing the immense privilege of being a mother to this beautiful soul. In an instant, my heart and soul transformed forever, intertwined with my boundless love for my newborn son.

I envisioned him living a vibrant life, excelling as a star athlete and valedictorian in high school. I pictured him graduating from college and marrying his high school sweetheart. Raising this boy will undoubtedly be my most outstanding achievement in life.

Then, the shift occurred that shattered my hopes when God's blessings started embracing this world's unrealistic ways of life. But I was reminded, *"In this world you will have trouble. But take heart! I have over the world"* (John 16:33).

My son became withdrawn and disrespectful. I dealt with his emotional outbursts, his getting into fights, and his late nights coming home.

I tried dealing with him by using my past methods to counteract this. First, I tried to ignore what I was seeing. Why? I was too busy and didn't want to deal with his issues. I assumed he would resolve whatever was bothering him on his own.

That approach didn't work, so I resorted to passing out punishments. No matter how many privileges I removed, he persisted in rebellion. So, next came the yelling. I knew this would do the trick. It didn't. My raised voice only further encouraged his negative behavior.

I did everything possible, but he refused to revert to the son I once knew.

My continual focus on my son caused me to lose relationships. My life revolved around him, leaving no room for myself.

Am I wrong to want him to be happy yet make healthy life decisions? It's heart-wrenching to accept that he plans to continue down a path that leads to more pain and disappointment.

Watching him continue to make bad choices left me torn between wanting him to learn the hard way and being afraid of what he might do in a moment of irresponsibility.

I was ready to give up, but that inner voice kept repeating, "There is still hope for your son."

One fate-filled evening

After dinner, my son informed me he was heading out for the night. At first, I was fine until he mentioned who would be joining him. The tension between us had already been building for days, and now he wants to hang out with a kid I recently forbade him from seeing. This drew my frustration to breaking, and I succumbed to the anger and hurt festering beneath the surface.

"Oh, no! You can't go!" I yelled.

His rebellious behavior escalated, pushing the boundaries of our already strained relationship. My living room turned into a boxing ring, and round one began.

We raised our voices and exchanged hurtful words. The once-peaceful atmosphere turned into a battlefield of raging emotions.

Tears streamed down my face as I struggled to maintain control and find a way to break through the walls he erected. No luck. We ended the night with hurtful threats thrown at one another.

In the aftermath, I retreated to my room. My heart was heavy with guilt, disappointment, and an overwhelming sense of powerlessness. I grieved the loss of the dreams I once had. That's when I realized I couldn't rescue him.

The decision to divorce his father haunted me, and I wondered if my choices had led to the rebellious son I now had to face alone. I internalized my emotions, leading to feelings of guilt and self-blame. I questioned whether I had done something wrong that contributed to his actions.

Desperate, I crawled out of bed and cried, "God. Seriously. I need HELP!" I begged Him not to let my son continue down this destructive path.

A False Sense of Peace

School let out that following week. He agreed to attend an out-of-state college summer camp for young engineers. This was the first time I could breathe in ages. I embraced the peace of his absence that settled in the house.

Two weeks later, on my way to work, I received a call from my mother. She was inquiring about my son. I told her that he wasn't returning my texts. I assumed everything was good because the school didn't call with any concerns.

We continued to chat, but she kept inquiring about his well-being. I finally realized she had something to say. She told me before my son left for camp how depressed he sounded. She was worried, so she contacted his best friend, my niece. He shared with them that he was mentally tired and no longer wanted to live. He planned to end his life after arriving at camp.

WHAT! I almost drove my car off the side of the road. Furiously. I said, "Mom. He's been at school for two weeks, and I haven't heard from him." She said, "I know. That is why I'm calling."

How dare she call weeks later after learning of his plan. Seriously? I had to check on my son. I called and left a threatening message. He texted back, asking me to call him after class.

I felt relieved. He was alive. Parked on the side of the road, the questions of why, how, and when flooded my head. I didn't know what to do next.

I am a faithful Christian who goes to church every Sunday. Why did God let this happen? How could this be? Will God protect other children but leave mine to fend for himself? At that moment, I started doubting my faith.

Forcing those thoughts not to dominate, I remembered how my boss took time off work last year because his daughter tried suicide. If anyone could relate to what I was feeling, he could.

Through the tears, I shared with him all I just learned. He said, drop everything and go right now and see about your son. I complained about the 4-hour drive and how it's already been two weeks. Again, he said, "GO to your son!"

I called my son again. I apologized for my tone in my earlier message and invited him to dinner. He agreed.

The drive there was so intense. I couldn't control the thoughts racing through my head: "My son is thinking about suicide? Did he already try it? Will he try again? Why didn't I know? Why didn't my mother tell me before he left for camp?"

I had no idea what to say that wouldn't lead to an argument. I cried out for God to tell me what to do. All I got back was silence.

I didn't want to show him my weariness. So, upon my arrival, I dusted away the tears and hid my shaking hands. Surprisingly, when he met me in the car, he smiled. I hadn't seen that in a long time. I decided now wasn't the best time to discuss the subject. Instead, I much preferred to enjoy the moment.

At dinner, excitement flowed as he described the school, his new friends, and how he couldn't wait to return next year. "Who is this kid?"

Later that evening, we decided to relax at the local park. As we sat enjoying the night air, my thoughts turned to the true purpose of my trip. Not noticing the slow stream of tears that began, I turned to him and said,

> "Son, I realize things have been tense between us lately. Please know that I care so much about you and your feelings. My world would be destroyed if you chose to leave it. I'm willing to start over if you are."

Based on his facial expression, I was uncertain about what he would say next. However, to my surprise, we embraced each other tightly for what felt like an eternity. He didn't ask how I knew, and I didn't tell. We just remained silent and allowed the moment to flow.

That Sunday at church, I went up for an altar call. My tears were my prayer. Suddenly, I felt a hand on my shoulder. I opened my eyes to see the Pastor. He grabbed my hand, and we started praying. His words were everything I needed to say to God.

Back in my car, I sat for what seemed like hours. Finally, I found the willpower to drive home. As I turned the key, I suddenly heard a voice say, *I know it's hard being a single mom. I will help.*

Knowing what I heard, I grabbed my phone and Googled, "I will help bible scripture." I found the following verse:

"So do not fear, for I am with you; do not be dismayed, for I am your God. I will strengthen you and help you; I will uphold you with my righteous right hand"
Isaiah 41:10.

God heard my prayer. He not only answered it; He came to help.

That word gave me the strength I never knew I had. That inner voice I heard all along was right. There is hope for my son.

I knew what I needed to do. At home, I got back into prayer. There, God equipped me with the tools *shared in the "Practical Solutions" section*, which shifted my attention to discovering his real issue. I stopped focusing on his behavior and started asking *WHY* he was acting this way.

My Son's Story Continues

When he returned home from camp, I noticed a change. There was a pleasant demeanor about him. That same smile continued. He was nicer to his brother and took part in family gatherings. He was not the same kid I dropped off at the start of camp.

I admit I enjoyed seeing my son in this new light. However, I couldn't shake the feeling of not knowing why he considered suicide. One evening after dinner, I went into his room.

This is what he had to say.

He expressed that he felt disappointed. The weight of his best friend moving away, the relentless harassment he endured at school, and the constant fights between us became too much to bear. The overwhelming pressure took its toll on him.

To escape this burden, he turned to drugs, influenced by the glamorized images he saw on social media. However, the bliss was short-lived because he hated how it made him feel. Still feeling lost, he found comfort in a group of like-minded friends despite knowing I disapproved of them.

One night, while he and his friends were spending time together, the topic of suicide arose. One of the kids pondered whether death might be preferable to living in constant sadness. At first, he didn't think much of it, but as the struggles continued, he began to entertain the same dark thoughts.

After our big blowout, he cried out to God, asking him to change his life. When he woke up the next morning feeling no different, he planned to end his life when he arrived at camp. Neither knew then, but we both separately prayed to God that night.

At camp, my son met a new friend who brought a spark of life into his world. This friend was unlike the others—vibrant and full of energy. They instantly connected and spent every moment together. Through this newfound friendship, he found a reason to wake up with renewed enthusiasm each day. The thoughts of suicide receded into the background until I visited with the conversation in the park.

"Why didn't you tell me how you were feeling?" I asked.

"You never had the time." He replied. We hugged, and I reassured him I would make the time.

I didn't realize that my son was feeling rejected. He wanted love and acceptance but wasn't getting it from home anymore. As a result, he began seeking it elsewhere through negative influences such as social media, peers, drugs, and alcohol. These outlets started to satisfy his unfulfilled desires, not knowing the harmful consequences of accepting their false truths.

As a result, he started rejecting those who loved him and gravitated towards the influencers who gave him attention. He did not willingly accept their false beliefs. He only desired their acceptance.

It took quite some time for me to come to terms with these thoughts until a moment of clarity came during my time in prayer. My son was right. I did put everything in front of our relationship. I was there without really being there for him. This life lesson was hard to learn, but I'm glad God stepped in to help when my son and I needed him the most. I didn't see Him in action, but we both experienced His results.

THOUGHTS TO PONDER

Prayer

Pray this prayer aloud.

"Lord, grant me strength and wisdom to navigate this difficult season. Help me see my son through your eyes and guide him with grace. Protect him from harm, surround him with positive influences, and soften his heart to hear your voice.

I surrender my fears and worries, trusting in your divine plan. Grant us reconciliation and healing in our relationship. Fill our interactions with love and understanding. I am grateful for the gift of motherhood, knowing that you walk beside me, providing strength.

In Jesus' name. Amen."

Scriptures

- "God is our refuge and strength, an ever-present help in trouble." (Psalm 46:1)
- "Trust in the Lord with all your heart and lean not on your own understanding; in all your ways submit to him, and he will make your paths straight." (Proverbs 3:5-6)
- "Come to me, all you who are weary and burdened, and I will give you rest. Take my yoke upon you and learn from me, for I am gentle and humble in heart, and you will find rest for your souls. For my yoke is easy and my burden is light." (Matthew 11:28-30)

Affirmations

- "I trust in God's plan and lean on His strength in all I do."
- "I embrace each day gracefully, knowing I am enough just as I am."
- "I am resilient and face challenges with courage and faith."

Practical Application

1. Begin each day with moments of prayer, reflection, and scripture reading. This sets a positive tone for the day ahead.
2. Take a few minutes daily to write down things you're grateful for about your son. This practice helps shift focus towards blessings and encourages a positive outlook.
3. Spend time outdoors in nature, appreciating God's creation. This can be a powerful way to feel connected with God.

Text your son this affirmation today.

I want you to know how incredibly special and loved you are. Your uniqueness is a gift to this world, and you have the strength and abilities to achieve anything you want.

CHAPTER 3

Ishmael's Story

"And as for Ishmael, I have heard you...
But my covenant I will establish with Isaac"
Genesis 17:20-21

The Bible contains several accounts depicting parents struggling to raise children who walk away from their parental-guided path. These narratives offer insights into the complexities of parenting troubled youths—stories such as.

The Parable of the Prodigal Son (Luke 15:11-32): This is one of the most famous stories in the Bible about a troubled youth and his father's response. A younger son asks for his inheritance and leaves home, only to squander his wealth in reckless living.

Eli and His Sons (1 Samuel 2:12-36; 1 Samuel 4): Eli was a priest with two sons, Hophni and Phinehas, known for their wickedness and disrespect towards God's commands. They committed various sins, including taking more than their share of offerings and engaging in immoral behavior.

Samson and His Parents (Judges 13-16): Samson's parents faced the unique challenge of raising a son with great strength and a divine calling. However, Samson's impulsive nature and poor decisions led him into conflict and trouble, particularly in his relationships with women.

The Bible shares a similar story of a parent's vision for their son shattered by their actions. I'm speaking of Abraham and his first-born son, Ishmael.

Their story teaches us about family, tough choices, and having faith in tough times. It points out the challenges of navigating love, responsibility, and divinely guided decisions amidst the complexities of human emotions.

Abraham – His Father _(Genesis 15-17, 21)_

God promised to bless Abraham and his descendants—making him the father of a great nation. However, his wife, Sarah, became increasingly impatient after years of waiting to conceive. She began to doubt that she was the one to help fulfill God's promise.

This era considered a wife's barrenness or childlessness as a social disaster. To avoid this, it was customary for husbands to take a maidservant. In desperation, Sarah suggested Abraham take her maidservant, Hagar, hoping to build their family through her. Abraham agreed.

Hagar gave birth to Ishmael in a tense environment due to her feelings of superiority, which led to mistreatment from Sarah.

Through all this, Abraham tried his best to be there for Ishmael. Abraham believed for thirteen years that his son was the rightful heir to his estate and the new land God promised him. He taught him important things about faith and being a good person.

God later revisited Abraham, vowing a covenant with his descendants. However, God said this covenant would only be with the child his wife Sarah would bear.

Being in his nineties, Abraham thought he and his wife were too old to conceive, so he asked God if Ishmael could live under this blessing. God agreed to bless Ishmael by making him fruitful, increasing his numbers, and a father to twelve rulers but clarified that the covenant would only go to Sarah's child.

Sarah soon bore a child, Isaac, as God had promised. However, the problems between the two women continued. Finally, Sarah demanded Abraham cast out Hagar and Ishmael so peace could resume in her home.

Abraham was torn with this decision because of his love for Sarah and Ishmael. He consulted God and grudgingly followed His command. With a heavy heart, he asked Hagar and Ishmael to leave, making them homeless.

Hagar – His Mother

An enslaved Egyptian, Hagar's troubles stemmed from other people's choices. Her pregnancy was marked with hope and difficulty. She endured constant mistreatment from her mistress after giving birth.

Her motherhood experience was intertwined with this relational tension, making her life a challenging struggle.

Hagar viewed Ishmael's birth as a sense of accomplishment and significance. She believed she contributed to God's promise to

Abraham, not Sarah. This new position she assumed she had obtained only strained her relationship with Sarah.

Trying to escape the mistreatment, Hagar ran away. Having no one to turn to, she was scared, alone, and with a child. In her despair, she received a visit from an Angel. He reassured her that God heard her in her misery and would help (Gen. 16:7). Hagar replied, "You are the God who sees me. I see now the One who sees me." (Gen. 16:13)

Hagar returned only to be kicked back out after the birth of Isaac. Hagar's experience as a mother was marked with despair as she wandered in the wilderness with her son, eventually leaving him alone under a bush because she did not want to face his death.

Hagar's encounter with an angel demonstrates the significance of faith even in the bleakest circumstances. Hagar's belief in the angel's guidance when she was at her lowest illustrates the comforting power of faith in a higher purpose, guiding us through the darkest moments of life.

Ishmael

Much of what happened throughout his life cannot be blamed on him. He found himself entangled in a process that was beyond his control.

Being Abraham's firstborn, Ishmael believed he held a special place in God's plan and that he would be the one to continue his father's legacy. However, Sarah's pregnancy must have started a downward spiral in understanding his place in the world. His confident self-esteem is now crushed.

Suddenly, his position as the presumed heir was undermined. His thoughts could have raced with questioning his self-worth, his purpose in life, and whether his role had been diminished. Struggling to accept his newfound secondary status within the family, he took this out on his brother Issac.

Then, the feeling of betrayal takes hold. First, his father forced him and his mother from the only home he knew. Then, after wandering the desert, his mother abandons him, leaving him to die.

He reached his breaking point, so He cried out to God. Even in this, God heard his cry. He sent an angel to Hagar to help get them through.

A Destructive Behavioral Lifestyle

Ishmael's upbringing emphasizes that parents' actions can significantly influence their children's self-perception. Growing up in a household full of conflict and witnessing the mistreatment between his mother and Sarah forced him to mentally navigate through their jealousy and abuse. His parents' confusion and displacement towards each other are experiences forever etched in his mind.

As parents, we often forget how our children get caught in the crossfire of our emotions. Parents fighting amongst themselves significantly impacts the child's thoughts and behaviors.

How? Children are susceptible to the emotional atmosphere in their homes, and conflicts between parents can leave lasting impressions that shape their development.

It's important to note that not all conflicts between parents negatively affect children. Constructive disagreements resolved with respect and effective communication can demonstrate healthy conflict-resolution skills. However, when conflicts escalate into frequent, intense, and unresolved fights, the potential for negative impacts on children's thoughts and behaviors increases.

For Ishmael, God already knew how his childhood would impact his life. We see this in the Book of Genesis 16:12 when the angel foretells Ishmael's adulthood to Hagar before his birth:

> *He will be a wild donkey of a man; his hand will be against everyone and everyone's hand against him, and he will live in hostility toward all his brothers.*
> —Genesis 16:12

The "wild donkey of a man" signifies that Ishmael would be free-spirited, untamed, and independent. The imagery of a wild donkey emphasizes his fierce and wild nature.

The subsequent phrase, "his hand will be against everyone and everyone's hand against him," suggests that Ishmael would have a contentious relationship with others and be involved in conflicts and disputes. It indicates a life marked by strife and discord.

The phrase ends with "he shall live in hostility toward all his brothers," which implies that Ishmael's descendants would live in conflict with the people around them, referring to the ongoing tensions between Ishmael's descendants, who became the Arab people and the descendants of Isaac, who became the Israelites.

The seeds planted during Ishmael's mental development harvested his adult rebellious behavior. We see this in Psalm 83:4-6:

> "Come," they say, "let us destroy them as a nation, so that Israel's name is remembered no more." With one mind they plot together; they form an alliance against you—the tents of Edom and the *Ishmaelites*, of Moab and the Hagrites.

The division between the two brothers – the son born by human will vs. the son born of a promise[1], sowed seeds of resentment in Ishmael that later fostered the desire in the Ishmaelites to eliminate Israel as a nation. That harvested hostility produced from Ishmael's childhood negatively impacted the future generations of the two sons.

God is Close to the Broken Hearted

God highlighted one thing throughout Ishmael's and my son's stories. He hears our misery and comes to help. In some way, Hagar and I fell short of protecting our sons, and yet God provided. He reminded me, *"The Lord is close to the broken-hearted and saves those who are crushed in spirit"* (Psalm 34:18).

My son found joy in a new friendship. Ishmael received reassurance from an angel by instructing Hagar to lift him and hold his hand.

He stood by them when they believed there was no way out and immediately rescued them from their struggles. God's intervention brings us a message that there is still hope.

Teenagers like my son and Ishmael exhibit rebellious behavior due to their interpretation of experiences. Let's learn more.

THOUGHTS TO PONDER

Prayer

Pray this prayer aloud.

Heavenly Father, please grant me the strength to continue when the road seems challenging and the wisdom to make the right decisions for my son. Help me to find solace in Your promises and to lean on Your unfailing love. Lord, please reassure me that a mother's role is meaningful and significant. When I feel over-looked or undervalued, remind me that You see me. You see the late nights, the sacrifices, the tears, and the joys. You see my efforts, and You love me just as I am.

As Hagar found hope and direction during her trials, I ask for Your guidance and provision in mine. Show me the way forward, lead me to places of security and peace, and help me trust in Your plan even when it's unclear.

Thank You for the beautiful reminder in Hagar's story that Your compassion knows no bounds. Please help me to extend that same compassion to myself and my son.

In Jesus' name, Amen."

Scriptures

- "So do not fear, for I am with you; do not be dismayed, for I am your God. I will strengthen you and help you; I will uphold you with my righteous right hand." (Isaiah 41:10)

- "He tends his flock like a shepherd: He gathers the lambs in his arms and carries them close to his heart; he gently leads those that have young." (Isaiah 40:11)
- "God is our refuge and strength, an ever-present help in trouble."(Psalm 46:1)

Affirmations

- "I am a capable and loving mother, equipped to manage any challenge that comes my way."
- "I embrace each moment with my children, cherishing the journey of motherhood."
- "A community of love and understanding supports me, and I am never alone in this journey."

Practical Application

1. Write in your journal the lesson you learned from this chapter.
2. Engage in biblical meditation to develop patience. Dedicate a few minutes daily to sitting in a quiet space while reading one of the above scriptures. Focus your reading on each word and allow the Holy Spirit to unlock their meaning to you. When your mind wanders, gently bring your attention back by rereading His words.
3. Surround yourself with a supportive community of other mothers, friends, or family members who understand the difficulties of parenting. Regularly connect with them to share experiences, seek advice, and provide mutual encouragement.

Text your son this affirmation today.

Remember that you can achieve greatness. Your determination and unique qualities will carry you far. I believe in you always.

Section Two

ATTAINING UNDERSTANDING

Attaining Understanding

*"Trust in the Lord with all your heart
and lean not on your own understanding;
in all your ways submit to him,
and he will make your paths straight."*
Proverbs 3:5-6

WHAT YOU WILL ATTAIN

The "Attaining Understanding" section dives into the underlying reasons behind our teenage sons' rebellious tendencies. This section thoroughly examines the adolescent mindset, presenting insightful revelations into how they perceive and engage with their environment.

By grasping the fundamental causes of their rebellious conduct, you will be equipped with knowledge and a greater appreciation to connect with your sons on a more compassionate level. This segment is an illuminating resource, shedding light on the intricate dynamics and enabling you further to comprehend your sons' distinct challenges and aspirations.

YOU'RE EQUIPPED TO FINISH THE RACE

"Do you not know that in a race all the runners run, but only one gets the prize? Run in such a way as to get the prize."
1 Corinthians 9:24

At the start of any race, all runners start strong, holding onto the same goal - to win.

The race unfolds, and the dedicated athletes settle into their pace with precision, while the unsteady steps of the distracted are a testament to their mixed emotions. Their form needs to have the grace and efficiency of a well-prepared athlete. Arms swing erratically, and steps are uneven, wasting precious energy —their gaze flickers from side to side, latching onto anything but the path ahead. The world around them blurs into a tapestry of indistinct shapes and sounds. Despite the chaos, there are moments when a glimmer of focus breaks through. A cheer from the sidelines momentarily grounds them, reminding them of the task. A fellow runner's encouraging nod ignites a spark of determination deep within. They find their stride, their body and mind coordinated momentarily.

To win this race, keep the end goal in mind (saving your son), know your opponent (what is he battling with), and pace yourself (trust God during the process).

However, many grow tired midway and need more time to finish. You, on the other hand, have the upper advantage. God is with you. He is that fellow runner, and I am your sideline cheerleader. No matter how tough the race appears, push forward until you reach the finish line.

"The race is not given to the strong one but to the one who can endure to the end" (Ecclesiastes 9:11). It doesn't matter how you start. What counts is how you finish. When you trust God, your latter will always be great.

CHAPTER 4

The Mindset of An Adolescent

Be made new in the attitude of your minds.
Ephesians 4:23

O ur mind is a powerful tool. It's not synonymous with the brain. The brain is the hardware that allows us to experience these mental states. Think of the mind as a vast puzzle of thoughts, feelings, and beliefs. The ideas we have can influence how we see things, how we feel, and how we act. When connected, they highlight our thoughts' crucial role in shaping our experiences.

Just as the wind is invisible yet sometimes powerful, so are your thoughts in the mind. As a man thinks in his heart, so is he (Proverbs 23:7 KJV). So, when does our mental development begin?

In The Beginning

Adolescence is crucial for developing social and emotional habits essential for mental well-being. Our sons acquire coping mechanisms, problem-solving abilities, and people skills here. It is also a key period for learning to manage emotions and behaviors.

Adolescent mindsets are particularly vulnerable to adversity, pressure to conform with peers, and exploration of identity. Remember your teenage years. It was not an easy journey. We went through significant physical, emotional, and social changes.

These years are a time of self-discovery and forming one's identity. It often means questioning everything around you, including rules and authority. So, when our sons challenge our decisions or express their opinions more vigorously, remind yourself that it's a part of their growth process.

My son's harvested behavior resulted from the constant clash between my words and those of the outside world, both fighting to take center stage. He was caught in a complex inner struggle as both sides fought to influence his behavior.

This clash between the two forces became intense. My son was torn between the comforting familiarity of my advice and the world's tempting promises of acceptance and popularity.

As he strove for independence, he grappled with reconciling his emerging identity, which led to inner conflicts, doubts, and at times, rebellion.

I find it challenging to make sense of this world today, so I can't imagine it from his eyes—no wonder many may struggle to discover what God created them to evolve into.

The Mind

"The mind of a man plans his ways."
Proverbs 16:9 NASB

Adolescence is a time of significant growth and development of our sons' minds. They begin questioning and analyzing information, typically weighing the pros and cons of a situation.

To understand this further, I'll dive deeper into how our mindset controls our behavior.

Indeed.com published an article outlining our cognitive processes in the conscious mind.[1]

The article tells how the Cognitive Process is our mind's conscious and unconscious thoughts involving self-awareness.

Cognitive processes are chemical and electrical signals in the brain that help you understand your surroundings, control your responses, and gain knowledge.

These processes include thinking, remembering, judging, and problem-solving. It controls our intellect, reason, and thoughts and forms our beliefs or judgments based on current or past experiences. Here is where our beliefs, values, and identity are shaped.

Imagine a bank - a secure place for storing, lending, exchanging, and protecting valuable currency. Similarly, our minds function as storage locations that evolve. For teenagers, their mental storage is constantly developing and receiving deposits as they grow more mature.

Deposit type #1: What's displayed at home. What model does he have to emulate? Is there a male model present at home? Whether good or bad, it is shown to him day and night.

Deposit type #2: Environment. This can be school or neighborhood—any outside influence.

Deposit type #3: Media / Social. The world's description of what a man should be. The media is excellent at bringing about curiosity and feeding it with what tastes good to the soul.

Deposit type #4: Who's in their ear? Friends and peers significantly impact a teenage boy's thoughts. They seek acceptance and belonging, often prioritizing peer opinions over others, including parental guidance.

These deposits of information are held and grow interest by establishing their imagination, memory, will, and sensation. After interest is acquired, a withdrawal is made - their behavior and personality.

They receive deposits that contribute to their behavior from many sources outside of our awareness. These are their *thoughts*, *perceptions*, and *memories*.

Thought

Not spoken aloud or expressed through any physical manifestation. Sometimes also referred to as our "inner voice." In short, they are verbalized language that exists only within our brains. The thoughts in their minds act like influencers, sometimes fueled by peer pressure, societal expectations, or a desire to explore and rebel. These thoughts may not always align with rational decision-making, especially when seeking a sense of identity or belonging.

Decision-making, problem-solving, and deductive and inductive reasoning are all examples of thoughts.

Perception

Perception occurs through the five senses: sight, taste, smell, sound, and touch. This cognitive process often consciously and unconsciously interprets information gained through our perceptions, forming thoughts, opinions, and emotional reactions. For instance, the smell of a particular flower may remind you of a specific person and bring back a pleasant memory.

Memory

Memory refers to the psychological processes of acquiring, storing, retaining, and later retrieving information. This collected information is stored in both our short-term and long-term memory.

> *Short-term memory*: The working memory. It consists of the information active in your consciousness, the things you're aware of.

Long-term memory: The memory process in the brain that takes information from the short-term memory store and creates lasting memories. Remember, *"Your mind will always believe everything you tell it"* *(unknown)*.

Other Mental Influencers

Social Interactions

Relationships have a strong influence on our behavior. People are more likely to make healthy choices when socially connected and have stable and supportive relationships. Creating social relationships is crucial for our well-being. When a person is socially isolated, they often experience feelings of loneliness.

"Young people who have poor relationships with peers are more likely to use drugs and engage in socially disruptive behaviors, report anxiety/depressive symptoms, have poorer adult relationships."[2]

Social interactions are proposed to be a basic human need. Its interactions are a dynamic platform for teenagers to develop cognitive skills, emotional intelligence, social competencies, and a sense of self. They learn to articulate their thoughts and emotions and adapt their communication style based on the context and audience.

Meaningful interactions with peers and adults shape their attitudes, values, and worldviews, influencing their personal growth and preparing them for successful engagement in various aspects of life. These interactions stimulate their critical thinking, problem-solving, and creativity.

Social Media

Social media platforms initially offered a canvas for creative self-expression, allowing teens to curate profiles highlighting various aspects of their personalities. It has evolved into a prominent platform for self-expression, but it also comes with its own set of complexities.

It often seems like the lives of those we follow are living their best life. People tend to share the highlights of their existence, displaying their achievements, beautiful moments, and exciting experiences, or often just a portrayal of their idealized version of reality. This selective sharing can create an illusion of constant positivity and success, which doesn't accurately reflect the full spectrum of real-life experiences.

Social media also presents various perspectives, opinions, and standards. The allure of likes, shares, and followers can create a strong pull, influencing a teenager's thoughts, desires, and self-esteem. Curated posts and glossy images can fuel aspirations but instigate feelings of inadequacy and the need to conform to societal norms.

It can also present a never-ending stream of exciting events and activities, leading users to experience fear of missing out when they feel they are missing experiences others share. This fear can make people feel dissatisfied with their own lives.

Studies have shown that social media can be more addictive than alcohol or cigarettes because the internet is free, easy to access, and available 24/7. It bombards us with messages about who we should be and what we should like if we want to be considered cool, accepted, or even popular.

His self-esteem is in constant comparison to an idealized version of others. It is vital to have open and honest conversations with him about his social media use and the impacts on his self-perception.

· · ·

Our Role

As mothers, we play a vital role in cultivating the mental and emotional traits within our sons, shaping their thoughts, emotions, and overall perspective on life. If left to interpret these traits alone, their mind might follow false ideas. We serve as their cornerstone by supplying essential emotional, social, and practical support to help him thrive.

To ensure they continue the guided path, we must aid in nurturing their self-confidence. Like lighthouses warning mariners of danger, you must nurture their minds to navigate the worldly exposures they meet daily. You are their compass. Help them to steer in the right direction.

Our sons struggle to choose between different influences, so we must help them navigate these challenges. We must give unwavering support and encouragement by providing a safe space for them to discover their interests, strengths, and passions. Our acceptance and understanding of their individuality, steered by our guidance, allow them to embrace their uniqueness and develop a sense of belonging. As they navigate life's complexities, our wisdom becomes their guiding light, offering perspective and empathy.

THOUGHTS TO PONDER

Prayer

Pray this prayer aloud.

"Thank you, Lord, for always being present in me and my teenage son's life. As I guide him through these years, I ask for Your guidance and strength. Lord, help him develop a mindset centered on You. Renew his thoughts and teach him to make choices that honor You.

Grant him wisdom to recognize thoughts aligned with Your will. Strengthen him to stand firm in his faith and resist worldly pressures. Remind him of Your closeness in tough times. Comfort him when he faces challenges. Thank you for the privilege of being his mother. May his mind reflect Your truth, and his thoughts show Your love.

In Jesus' name. Amen."

Scriptures

- "How can a young person stay on the path of purity? By living according to your word." (Psalm 119:9)
- "But those who hope in the Lord will renew their strength. They will soar on wings like eagles; they will run and not grow weary, they will walk and not be faint." (Isaiah 40:31)
- "God is our refuge and strength, an ever-present help in trouble." (Psalm 46:1)

Affirmations

- "I believe in the strength and resilience within my son, and I am here to support him every step of the way."
- "I am a steadfast and loving mother, seeking God's wisdom in nurturing my son's journey."
- "I trust in God's plan for my son's life, knowing His love and guidance are always with him."

Practical Application

1. Write in your journal the lesson you learned from this chapter.
2. Begin tomorrow with reflections on the good things your son has done in the past.
3. Breathing exercises can help you to manage stress and anxiety. Try the following exercise today. Take a deep, slow breath through your nose for a count of 4 seconds. Hold your breath for a count of 7 seconds. Then, slowly exhale through your mouth for a count of 8 seconds.

Text your son this affirmation today.

Think of a good time you had with your son and share that memory with him.

CHAPTER 5
A Healthy Mindset

"A healthy outside starts from the inside."
Robert Urich

Whether you are religious, spiritual, or none of the above, we all can agree on the importance of maintaining a healthy mindset.

To understand the term "Healthy Mindset," we must break out each word.

Healthy = Showing physical, mental, or emotional well-being.

Mindset = A mental attitude that determines how you interpret and respond to situations.

Therefore, a *Healthy Mindset* means having a balanced physical, mental, and emotional foundation that fosters growth, positivity, and a harmonious approach to life's complexities. People with a healthy mindset exhibit strong self-confidence and maintain a positive self-image. They show emotional well-being and can effectively manage and express their emotions.

How we think and feel about things determines how we manage stress, relate to others, and make choices.

Your feelings, actions, and relationships are good when you're mentally healthy. You can positively manage your thoughts, feelings, and behaviors. You can cope with the challenges and stresses of life constructively and adaptively.

God also lets us know the importance of having a healthy mindset. The Bible teaches us how to contribute to our mind's well-being and resilience, promoting good mental health.

Philippians 4:8: "Finally, brothers and sisters, whatever is true, whatever is noble, whatever is right, whatever is pure, whatever is lovely, whatever is admirable—if anything is excellent or praiseworthy—think about such things."

Philippians 4:6-7: "Do not be anxious about anything, but in every situation, by prayer and petition, with thanksgiving, present your requests to God. And the peace of God, which transcends all understanding, will guard your hearts and your minds in Christ Jesus."

1 Peter 5:7: "Cast all your anxiety on him because he cares for you."

Isaiah 26:3: "You will keep in perfect peace those whose minds are steadfast because they trust in you."

Facts and Stats

In 2019, the National College Health Assessment (NCHA)[1] noted that students reported feeling exhausted, lonely, and overwhelmed, among other symptoms and difficulties. Of the surveyed students, 20.2% reported experiencing depression, and 27.8% reported experiencing anxiety that affected their studies the preceding year.

Globally, an estimated 14% of ten to nineteen-year-olds experience mental health conditions that often go unrecognized and untreated.

Depression, anxiety, and behavioral disorders are among the leading causes of illness and disability among adolescents.

The consequences of failing to address adolescent mental health conditions extend to adulthood, impairing physical and psychological health and limiting opportunities to lead fulfilling lives.

Effects of An Unhealthy Mindset

Distorted thoughts and beliefs are the root of many behavior problems. Unhealthy thinking creates negative self-talk, convincing our sons they are incapable and prolonging suffering, leading to unpleasant emotions. The combination of negative thoughts and feelings may prompt them to escape or self-medicate with drugs, alcohol, food, sex, and other risky behaviors.

Unhealthy thinking can be a sign of poor mental health. Here are some adverse effects of toxic thinking that our sons may experience.

. . .

Destress, Disorder, and Disease

Let's talk about the critical connection between stressors, disorders, and diseases in the context of your teenager's mind. Imagine their mind as a delicate balance, like a finely tuned instrument. When stressors pile up, whether from school, relationships, or personal expectations, it can create disharmony within their mental and emotional well-being. This disharmony might lead to disorders like glitches in the system – things like anxiety, depression, or self-infliction. Just as a physical ailment can impact the body, these disorders can affect the mind.

Unchecked, these conditions can potentially manifest as more serious mental health diseases. Think of it as a minor leak turning into a bigger problem. That's why open communication and support are vital.

The mind, burdened by its unrelenting storm, cascades into a state of distress, a sea of chaos and disorder. Here, the delicate balance of mental well-being is disrupted, and disease manifestations take root. The resilient family stands as a lighthouse amidst the tumultuous waves, offering solace and support as they navigate the treacherous waters.

You are crucial in helping them maintain their mental well-being by promoting healthy coping mechanisms and seeking professional help. Just as you would promptly address a physical ailment, addressing mental health concerns early can significantly impact their overall health and happiness.

. . .

Malnutrition

Imagine their brain as a high-performance engine, constantly running and demanding optimal power. Malnutrition, like using poor-quality fuel, can impede their cognitive abilities, emotional well-being, and overall mental health. Just as their body needs balanced nutrition for growth and vitality, their mind requires essential nutrients to navigate the challenges of adolescence.

Inadequate nutrition can contribute to mood swings and lack of focus and even impact their ability to cope with stress. By providing a well-balanced diet rich in nutrients, you're nurturing their mind's resilience and ensuring it operates at its best. Additionally, fostering a healthy relationship with food and promoting regular meals can positively influence their self-esteem and body image, further bolstering their mental well-being. Your guidance in this aspect of their life can make a remarkable difference in their psychological and physical health.

The mind, entangled within the confines of its singular mindset, starves for nourishment. It craves the sustenance of positive thoughts, uplifting interactions, and the warmth of genuine connection. With hearts outstretched, the family provides nutrition through understanding, empathy, and unwavering love.

Misjudgment and Misguidance

Teenagers' misjudgment and misguided actions can often stem from the thoughts swirling in their minds. Think of their minds as a canvas on which various thoughts and emotions are painted. During adolescence, the mind undergoes significant development and transformation. If they follow false beacons, they can succumb to misjudgment and misguided beliefs.

It's crucial to recognize that these misjudgments and misguided actions often arise from a combination of factors, including a developing sense of self, hormonal changes, and the impact of external influences. We must offer guidance to illuminate the path forged through unity and collective strength.

False Directions

Imagine their minds as a vast landscape with many different pathways, each representing a choice or movements they can take. During adolescence, the allure of false directions becomes particularly strong. Their tempting shortcuts promise excitement or fulfillment but may lead them astray from their actual goals.

Teenagers sometimes draw toward false directions through peer pressure, societal trends, or the desire to stand out in their quest for independence and identity. These directions might seem appealing, fueled by thoughts that promise instant gratification or acceptance. However, these paths often lead to disappointment or negative consequences like a mirage in the desert.

As a guiding force, you help them differentiate between genuine opportunities and false directions. Engaging in open conversations about their aspirations, values, and the potential outcomes of different choices can help them navigate this maze of possibilities. By fostering critical thinking and self-awareness, you empower them to evaluate their thoughts and make decisions that align with their long-term well-being. Your wisdom and guidance function as a compass, steering them away from false directions and towards paths that lead to growth, happiness, and success.

Insecurities

Picture their minds as a fragile ecosystem where thoughts and emotions interweave to create a unique self-image. During adolescence, insecurities often cast a shadow over this mental landscape, influencing how they perceive themselves and interact with the world. Insecurities, which are like those nagging doubts we all have, can grow stronger in this storm. It's like feeling unsure and not valuing yourself.

Insecurities are like whispered doubts that echo in their minds, distorting their self-perception and coloring their interactions. These thoughts may stem from societal standards, peer comparisons, or firsthand experiences. Insecurities can lead to various behaviors, from seeking validation to withdrawing from social situations. They can also drive them to make decisions based on fear rather than genuine desires.

Your role as their nurturing guide involves helping them address and manage their insecurities. Providing a supportive environment where they feel comfortable discussing their feelings is crucial. Through open conversations, you can help them challenge negative self-perceptions and develop a more balanced view of themselves. Encourage them to focus on their strengths and passions, fostering a sense of self-worth that isn't solely reliant on external validation. By helping them navigate their insecurities, you're fostering resilience and empowering them to make choices based on their true potential rather than their doubts.

Rejection

Teenagers face rejection daily. When they feel unloved, they may be at a higher risk of developing mental health problems, such as depression, anxiety, or mood disorders. We often don't realize teenagers' emotional challenges when seeking love and acceptance from essential people who matter most to them. Due to their ongoing brain development, they may struggle to process their thoughts and emotions. As a result, when faced with rejection, they may experience difficulties with emotional regulation and social cognition, making it hard to know how to behave.

It is not unusual for teenagers to encounter emotional difficulties, especially rejection-related ones. Significant emotional and psychological changes occur during adolescence; various elements can influence how teenagers handle rejection. As a result, teenagers may feel anxious and depressed, have low self-esteem, and withdraw socially.

Feeling unloved by one's mother can have significant emotional consequences for a teenager. A mother's love and support are crucial for a child's emotional well-being and healthy development. When a teenager perceives or experiences a lack of love from their mother, it can lead to various emotional challenges.

Self-Infliction

It is when one intentionally harms one's body without meaning for the injury to be fatal. It can offer insight into the complex emotions and struggles that young minds go through. Teenagers with self-inflicted wounds deal with intense emotions they might not fully understand. They use this coping method to manage distress, anger, and other painful emotions.

At times, self-infliction can arise as a desperate attempt to gain a semblance of control amidst chaos or as a manifestation of deeply buried emotions seeking release.

Remember, it's not a reflection of your parenting; it's about the complex journey of growing up and navigating emotions. If you notice signs of self-infliction or suspect your teenager might struggle, approach them with empathy, patience, and an open heart. Your support and guidance can make a positive difference in their emotional well-being.

The more risk factors teenagers experience, the more it can affect their mental health. Factors contributing to stress during adolescence include exposure to adversity, pressure to conform with peers and exploration of identity. Media influence and gender norms can exacerbate the disparity between an adolescent's lived reality and their perceptions or aspirations for the future. Other essential determinants include the quality of their home life and peer relationships. Violence (especially sexual violence and bullying), harsh parenting, and severe socioeconomic problems are recognized risks to mental health.

Our Role

As his mother, you can provide invaluable support for your son's unhealthy mindset by creating a safe and open environment for him to express his emotions without judgment. Actively listen, empathize, and validate his feelings, reinforcing his sense of self-worth and love. Consistent communication reminds him of his strengths, talents, and unique qualities, helping him regain confidence and perspective.

Work to strengthen your bond and offer a sense of belonging by engaging in shared activities and spending quality time together. Encourage him to explore his passions, build resilience, and develop coping strategies. These steps will instill in him a sense of empowerment and the understanding that emotions do not define his value.

Obtaining A Healthy Mindset

When our sons make hasty decisions, it's as if a storm is brewing inside their heads. Clear thinking becomes hard. It can lead them to feel overwhelmed and disorganized.

Our role as mothers is pivotal in helping them quiet the storm by giving them the tools to help assess their thoughts and emotions.

The tools to provide are fostering open conversations, actively listening, and having non-judgmental discussions. When applied correctly, they empower our sons to make healthier choices that align with your values.

Through all of this, a mother is like a shield, a source of strength and love. She stands by the person, helping through the tough times and showing she cares. Together, they face the storm and work toward healing and growth. Families are like a rope of truth, pulling them back to what is real and offering hope.

As the storm begins to clear, understanding starts to shine through. A mother's support and love make a real difference. Soon, her son isn't stuck in that one way of thinking. The family emerges stronger, connected by their journey through challenges, kindness, and unbreakable bonds.

THOUGHTS TO PONDER

Prayer

Pray this prayer aloud.

"Dear Lord, I ask for your divine guidance and comfort as he navigates the feelings that weigh heavily on his heart. Please grant me the wisdom to be a source of unwavering support and understanding. Help me create a safe space where he can openly share his thoughts and emotions without fear of judgment. May my words and actions reflect your love, reminding him of his inherent worth and the unique gifts you have bestowed upon him. Fill his spirit with courage and resilience and help him understand that he is cherished and valued beyond measure.

In Jesus' name. Amen."

Scriptures

- "For I know the plans I have for you, declares the Lord, plans to prosper you and not to harm you, plans to give you hope and a future." (Jeremiah 29:11)
- "Come to me, all you who are weary and burdened, and I will give you rest."(Matthew 11:28)
- "God is our refuge and strength, an ever-present help in trouble." (Psalm 46:1)

Affirmations

- I am a source of unwavering love and support for my son.

- I help my son see his strengths and remind him of his worth.
- I trust that our bond is strong, and I am committed to helping my son thrive in every aspect of his life.

Practical Application

1. Write in your journal the lesson you learned from this chapter.
2. Reflecting on what you learned, note any changes you observed in his behavior, mood, or habits that might indicate he's struggling.
3. Consider how your son might be experiencing some situations. Put yourself in his shoes and try to understand the emotions he's going through. Journal your thoughts.

Text your son this affirmation today.

You are worthy of love and acceptance. Embrace your uniqueness and know that you have valuable qualities to offer.

Section Three

PRACTICAL SOLUTIONS

The Practical Solutions

"And we know that in all things God works for the good of those who love him, who have been called according to his purpose."
Romans 8:28

You have arrived at the final part of this journey. Know that you're taking meaningful steps towards your son's success.

Before we begin, please take a moment to reflect on what you have learned in the earlier sections. It's okay if you need some time to process the information. If so, I suggest reviewing your notes and praying for further understanding. Once you are ready to continue, grab your journal. You will need it for this next section.

In this section, you will discover seven divinely inspired solutions to deliver tangible, workable results. Each is tailored to transform his self-perception.

Hopefully, now that you have found a reason for his rebellion. Focus on that while reviewing each solution in this section.

Here are the seven solutions you'll be reviewing.

1. **Nurturing Healthy Self-Esteem:** How to embrace his uniqueness and face challenges with confidence and resilience through our support and belief in them.

2. **Cultivating a Supportive Environment:** How to provide a stable foundation for growth where he can recognize his unique strengths and counter negative self-perceptions.

3. **Increasing in the Fruit of the Spirit:** How to tap into God's nine characteristics as a guiding framework for increasing your bond with your son.

4. **Facing the Man in the Mirror:** How do you allow God to reveal your son's genuine esteem through love and tenderness.

5. **Understanding The Five Love Languages:** How to identify your son's love language to better your relationship.

6. **Opening Lines of Communication:** Will identify how to develop an effective way to communicate with your son.

7. **Maintaining Unity:** How to create and maintain mutual agreement.

I've also included guided prayers following each solution. May God accompany you on your journey ahead.

CHAPTER 6

Nurturing Healthy Self-Esteem

"I praise you because I am fearfully and wonderfully made;
your works are wonderful, I know that full well."
Psalm 139:14

God created us in His image, intricately and wonderfully made. However, we often fail to embrace our uniqueness as a reflection of God.

In the ever-changing landscape of parenthood, one of our most profound responsibilities as mothers is to empower and nurture our children, helping them navigate the challenges and joys of life with strength, resilience, and a healthy sense of self-worth. As our sons transition into their tumultuous teenage years, they face unique trials and tribulations, chief among them being the development of confident self-esteem.

During adolescence, our sons start to acknowledge their abilities and their flaws. To develop a positive self-image, they require nurturing and guidance that encourages them to embrace their individuality.

Unfortunately, I did not provide adequate guidance to my son in this area, causing him to seek validation from external sources. He started to believe what society expected of him because I did not encourage him to believe in himself. This led to his struggle with low self-esteem.

When our sons experience low self-esteem, they may struggle with negative self-perceptions. They may internalize the negative opinions of others and view them as facts. This is often due to a lack of recognition of their unique qualities and worth.

As mothers, it is our role to nurture our children's gifts and talents, helping them to thrive and appreciate the abilities that they have been blessed with. This can boost their self-esteem and confidence.

The Foundations of Self-Esteem

In nurturing healthy self-esteem in our sons, it is crucial to begin at the core - understanding the foundations upon which their sense of self-worth is built. Self-esteem is not a fleeting emotion but a deep-seated belief in one's inherent value and worthiness. It is the sturdy pillar upon which a fulfilling, confident life is constructed.

At its essence, self-esteem comprises two fundamental components: self-worth and self-acceptance. Self-worth, akin to the bedrock of a sturdy structure, is the unshakeable belief that one is valuable and deserving of love, respect, and opportunities. It is the unspoken assurance that we are worthy of life's good things. Conversely, self-acceptance is embracing oneself with all their strengths, weaknesses, and imperfections. It acknowledges that they are flawed yet no less deserving of love and respect.

Together, these elements form the cornerstone upon which healthy self-esteem is constructed.

Recognizing Signs of Low Self-Esteem

1. Feeling unloved and unwanted

Feeling unloved and unwanted emotions often stem from a perception of inadequacy or a belief that he isn't deserving of affection or acceptance.

When someone grapples with low self-esteem, he may internalize negative feelings about himself, leading to a sense of unworthiness. This can profoundly affect their well-being, relationships, academic performance, and personal development.

How You Can Help

Help him recognize his inherent value and capabilities by addressing his feelings with empathy, understanding, and support. Encouraging self-love and affirming his worth as a unique and valuable individual can be pivotal in fostering a healthier self-esteem and a more positive outlook on life.

2. Blaming others for their own mistakes

This behavior often arises from a reluctance to confront their shortcomings and a fear of taking responsibility for their actions.

Individuals with low self-esteem tend to internalize a negative self-image, making it difficult to acknowledge their imperfections. Instead, they may deflect blame onto others as a means of self-preservation.

How You Can Help

Approach this behavior with sensitivity and understanding. Encourage open communication about feelings of self-worth and offer support to build a more positive self-image. By helping your son recognize and value his capabilities, you can work towards fostering a healthier sense of self-esteem and a greater understanding of personal accountability.

3. Can't deal with frustration

Minor setbacks or challenges can feel disproportionately overwhelming when one lacks confidence in one's abilities. This may lead to feelings of inadequacy and a sense of being unable to measure up to what is expected.

How You Can Help

Approach this situation with compassion and patience, providing a safe space for your son to express his feelings and offering guidance on managing frustration. By helping him build resilience and self-assurance, you can empower him to face difficulties more confidently, working towards a stronger self-esteem and a more positive outlook on his capabilities.

4. *Fear of failure or embarrassment*

When they lack confidence in their abilities, the prospect of making a mistake or facing public scrutiny can become a paralyzing source of anxiety. This fear often arises from a deep-seated belief that any misstep will further erode their sense of self-worth.

How You Can Help

Approach this situation with empathy and understanding, creating an environment where your son feels supported and encouraged to take risks. You can gradually nurture stronger self-esteem and greater resilience in facing challenges by helping him recognize that setbacks are a natural part of growth and learning. This will enable him to face potential failures with a healthier perspective, fostering a more positive self-image.

5. *Low levels of motivation and interest*

When someone lacks confidence in their abilities, they may struggle to find enthusiasm or purpose in their pursuits. This can lead to a diminished sense of self-worth, making it challenging to engage wholeheartedly in activities or set and pursue goals.

How You Can Help

Approach this situation with sensitivity and encouragement, helping your son discover his strengths and interests. You can gradually bolster his self-esteem by fostering an environment that supports his passions and offering positive reinforcement. As he begins recognizing his value and capabilities, we expect increased motivation and a renewed sense of purpose in his endeavors.

6. Can't take compliments. Show mixed feelings of anxiety or stress.

Acknowledging positive feedback can feel uncomfortable or unwarranted when they lack confidence in their worth. This may be accompanied by a heightened sensitivity to perceived judgment or criticism, leading to increased anxiety or stress levels.

How You Can Help

Approach this situation with empathy and reassurance, creating a space where our son feels safe and valued. We can gradually help him internalize a more positive self-image by actively affirming his achievements and reinforcing his self-worth. This, in turn, can reduce his anxiety and stress levels, contributing to a healthier sense of self-esteem and a more remarkable ability to accept compliments graciously.

The Role of Mothers in Shaping Self-Esteem

"Two are better than one because they have a good return for their labor: If either of them falls down, one can help the other up. But pity anyone who falls and has no one to help them up."
Ecclesiastes 4:9-10

This verse highlights the power of support, emphasizing the value of standing together through challenges and being there for each other in times of need.

As mothers, we hold an extraordinary power to shape the foundation of our sons' self-worth and confidence. Our words, actions, and unconditional love create an indelible mark on their hearts. A son's sense of self-esteem first takes root within the embrace of motherhood.

From the earliest moments of infancy, a mother becomes the first image a child sees. In our eyes, they find their reflection, not just in the physical sense but in the affirmation of their worthiness and belonging. Through tender gazes and gentle caresses, we communicate a message: "You are cherished, you are valued, and you are enough."

This initial connection lays the groundwork for their perception of self, setting the stage for a lifelong journey of self-discovery and self-affirmation. Our role as mothers is not merely one of caretakers but also nurturers, mentors, and unwavering sources of love and support. We are the architects of their self-esteem, crafting a sanctuary of confidence in which they can flourish.

Help your son fortify this foundation, ensuring he stands firm in life's challenges and uncertainties. Reiterate your love and acceptance for him, regardless of achievements or shortcomings. Let him know you value him for simply being himself.

How You Can Help

Communication Strategies for Building Confidence

Communication is more than words; it's about the quality of connection we foster. It involves active listening, empathetic responses, and nurturing an environment where our children feel safe expressing themselves. It's about not just talking but truly understanding and being understood. As mothers, we are the primary architects of these conversations, and it's our responsibility to shape them in a way that reinforces our son's self-worth.

Encourage Independence and Autonomy

Bestow upon your son the confidence to stand independently, make decisions, and chart their course in life. Encourage his independence by equipping him with the tools to become self-assured and capable.

Cultivate His Strengths and Interests

Encourage your son to explore his passions, which will help him develop skills and build a keen sense of self-worth. As you see him become enthusiastic about something, his belief in his abilities will grow, and laying a foundation will increase his confidence.

Promote Body Positivity and Self-Care
Teach your son to love and appreciate his body. Help cultivate a positive body image, encourage healthy habits, and provide the tools for him to navigate societal pressures gracefully and confidently. By nurturing a sense of self-worth that transcends physical appearance, we equip our children with the armor they need to face the world confidently and authentically.

Navigate Challenges Together
Walk alongside your son through the difficulties, offering our support, wisdom, and unwavering love. Your presence and actions demonstrate that challenges are not to be faced in isolation but as a team.

Provide Reassurance
Remind your son that asking for help and support is okay when needed. Assure him that seeking assistance or guidance is a sign of strength, not weakness.

Seek Professional Help if Needed
If you notice that your son is struggling with self-awareness or dealing with complex emotions, consider seeking the guidance of a child therapist or counselor. They can provide specialized support.

Obtaining A Healthy Self-Esteem

Improving one's self-esteem is a worthwhile task—what better way to achieve this than through a focused group activity?

Boosting our sons' confidence can be a wonderful bonding experience for a mother and her son.

Group exercises with your son are an excellent way to strengthen your bond and improve your physical health. It can also create a supportive and enjoyable atmosphere for bonding. Participating in shared experiences can help your son's self-confidence grow while instilling a sense of belonging and achievement.

Here are some group activities you can do together. Remember to create an atmosphere of support, encouragement, and non-judgment during these activities. This will help foster a positive environment for your son to build his self-esteem.

1. **Compliment Jar**: Create a jar filled with written compliments and positive affirmations. Take turns pulling out notes and reading them aloud to each other.
2. **Goal Setting and Achievement**: Sit down together and set achievable short-term and long-term goals. Celebrate accomplishments, no matter how small.
3. **Collaborative Art or Craft Project**: Engage in a creative endeavor like painting, drawing, or building something together. Praise each other's creativity and effort.
4. **Cooking or Baking Together**: Prepare a meal or bake a treat as a team. Encourage each other's efforts and enjoy the delicious results.
5. **Outdoor Adventure:** Go for a hike, bike ride, or participate in an outdoor activity you both enjoy. Overcoming physical challenges together can build confidence.

6. **Volunteer Work**: Choose a community service project and work together to make a positive impact. This reinforces a sense of purpose and accomplishment.
7. **Team Sports or Games**: Engage in a sport together requiring cooperation and teamwork. Encourage each other's contributions and celebrate successes.
8. **Positive Affirmation Exercise**: Take turns giving and receiving affirmations. Express specific things you appreciate about each other.
9. **Read and Discuss Inspirational Stories**: Choose books or articles with uplifting messages. Read them together and discuss the lessons learned.
10. **Role Reversal**: Take turns pretending to be each other and share positive qualities and accomplishments about the other person.

When you invest time in helping increase his self-esteem, you nurture a foundation for his overall well-being and success. By fostering a positive self-image, you equip him with the confidence to face life's challenges.

A mother's investment in her son's self-esteem strengthens their bond and empowers him to thrive as a capable and resilient individual.

Prayer

Pray this prayer aloud.

"Heavenly Father, I seek your guidance in nurturing and uplifting my beloved son. Grant me the wisdom to recognize his unique gifts and the strength to affirm his worthiness. May he know that he is fearfully and wonderfully made in your image.

Lord, help me lead by example, showing him the confidence that comes from knowing you. Let him see in me a reflection of self-assuredness. I entrust my son to your loving care, knowing you are the ultimate source of his identity and self-worth.

In Jesus name, Amen."

CHAPTER 7

Cultivating a Supportive Environment

One day, I sensed Jesus saying to me, *Create an environment where he'll feel valued, supported, and empowered, and watch him bloom beyond imagination.*

When God asked me to create a supportive environment for my son, I must admit I did not know how. I knew he needed a nurturing space where he felt appreciated, understood, and enabled, but I was unsure how to provide it.

Teenage boys, especially those going through rebellious phases, are experiencing a whirlwind of emotions. Providing a supportive home will give them a stable foundation where they feel safe expressing themselves and dealing with their feelings.

This supportive space doesn't mean avoiding discipline or consequences for their negative behavior. It means approaching the matter fairly and constructively while maintaining a foundation of love, trust, and open communication.

When I asked God for His help, He went straight to work. While He is fixing the issue at its root, the home needs to be a safe space where he can release what's troubling.

Still unsure how to fulfill Jesus' request, I delved into His Word to learn how to create this supportive environment. Here are the verses I discovered that helped me establish a welcoming home environment for my son.

1) "Carry each other's burdens, ..." (Galatians 6:2)

This verse taught me the significance of paying attention to my son's struggles and challenges. I realized that I should actively listen to him when he wants to speak and support him by offering help whenever he faces difficulty or hardship.

To adopt this verse, I took the following practical steps:

I decided to make my son feel comfortable enough to discuss anything on his mind after dinner. To build his trust, I wore a silly hat. I chose this hat for two reasons - first, it creates a light-hearted atmosphere. Next, I let him know he could confide in me without fear of judgment whenever I wore the hat.

Initially, my son found the hat ridiculous, but I continued to pursue the idea. Eventually, my persistence paid off. He began talking about a concern he had. It was a wonderful surprise to learn that he finally felt a sense of trust in me.

This approach fostered a supportive environment where he felt valued, understood, and empowered to express his feelings by confidently telling what was in his heart.

Action Item

What is one thing you can do to help your son feel safe to share what's on his heart?

_____

_____

2) *"Therefore encourage one another and build each other up, just as in fact you are doing."* (1 Thessalonians 5:11)

This verse taught me the importance of regularly encouraging my son with supportive words and appreciation to motivate his thinking.

To adopt this verse, I took the following practical steps:

Each day, I made it a point to send him words of encouragement that highlighted his value as a Kingdom King in my eyes and the eyes of God. These daily affirmations aimed to remind him of his inherent worth and capabilities. I intended to empower him to approach each day with confidence and strength.

Action Item

What can you do to encourage your son today that will build him up?

_____

_____

3) "Therefore, as God's chosen people, holy and dearly loved, clothe yourselves with compassion, kindness, humility, gentleness, and patience. Bear with each other and forgive one another if any of you has a grievance against someone. Forgive as the Lord forgave you. And over all these virtues put on love, which binds them all together in perfect unity." (Colossians 3:12-14)

This verse offers more than one way to provide a supportive environment:

- Embrace Compassion and Kindness
- Cultivate Humility and Gentleness
- Practice Patience and Bearing with Each Other
- Forgiveness as a Foundation
- Overarch Virtue of Love

This verse taught me to embody these virtues that would create a supportive environment where my son feels loved, valued, and empowered to grow into the person he is meant to become.

To adopt this verse, I took the following practical steps:

We agreed to let him choose and help prepare our Thursday night meals. This small gesture of kindness created a space for him to feel loved because we could engage in this joint activity together.

Action Item
What can you do today to make your son feel loved using one of the above virtues?

_____

_____

*4) "A generous person will prosper; whoever refreshes others will be refreshed." (*Proverbs 11:25)

This verse taught me the importance of generosity. I must teach my son how to share his time, resources, and talents with others. His acts will instill a sense of compassion and empathy, creating a supportive atmosphere.

To adopt this verse, I took the following practical steps:

During one of our recent dinner side discussions – Surprising, he asked me to wear my hat; we talked about ways he could use his talents to assist others. Allowing him to choose, he signed up for an after-school tutoring program for younger kids. I thanked him for his willingness to support someone else.

Action Item
What is one thing you can do to encourage your son to use his gifts and talents?

_____

_____

*5) "Start children off on the way they should go, and even when they are old they will not turn from it." (*Proverbs 22:6)

This verse taught me to examine myself. What was I instructing my son about the way he should go?

To adopt this verse, I took the following practical steps:

After attending church, I thought of a clever idea to use our drive time home to continue discussing what we learned. By sharing our thoughts, I can help ensure he remembers God's teachings and can refer to them when needed.

Action Item

What is one thing you can do to instill God's Word in your son?

_____

_____

6) *"And let us consider how we may spur one another on toward love and good deeds, not giving up meeting together, as some are in the habit of doing, but encouraging one another— and all the more as you see the Day approaching."* (Hebrews 10:24-25)

This verse taught me to keep my word when I commit to do something with him.

To adopt this verse, I took the following practical steps:

My son's favorite extracurricular activity is playing in his school's marching band. Despite my promise to attend all his games, there were times when work obligations prevented me from being there. To support him as best I could, I committed only to the games I knew I could attend.

Action Item

What commitment can you honor that would bring him joy?

_____

_____

7) *"We who are strong ought to bear with the failings of the weak and not to please ourselves. We should please our neighbors for their good, to build them up."* (Romans 15:1-2)

This verse taught me to celebrate his accomplishments, big or small.

To adopt this verse, I took the following practical steps:

My son and I didn't communicate much, so I was unaware of his accomplishments. Therefore, I decided to find at least one. His teacher informed me that he had passed his last exam, so I celebrated that victory with ice cream. This simple recognition encouraged him to start sharing his achievements with me, and we celebrated each one.

Action Item
What accomplishment has your son achieved that you can celebrate him for it?

_____

_____

8) *"Therefore confess your sins to each other and pray for each other so that you may be healed. The prayer of a righteous person is powerful and effective."* (James 5:16)

This verse taught me never to stop praying for my son.

To adopt this verse, I took the following practical steps:

While praying, I repented to God for stopping my prayers for my son and recommitted to continue praying for his deliverance, believing, by faith, that I will see it.

GOD, I'M WORRIED ABOUT MY SON

Action Item
Can you resume daily prayers and believe, by faith, for your son's deliverance?

_____

_____

9) *"Be kind and compassionate to one another, forgiving each other, just as in Christ God forgave you."* (Ephesians 4:32)

This verse taught me to be kind and forgive quickly when my son and I clashed.

To adopt this verse, I took the following practical steps:

I made a promise to myself not to react immediately after a disagreement. Instead, I will remain quiet, count to ten, and then express my thoughts. Although it was tough at first, it eventually became easier.

Action Item
What step of kindness can you show that will lead you towards forgiveness for your son?

_____

_____

10) *"So that there should be no division in the body, but that its parts should have equal concern for each other. If one part suffers, every part suffers with it; if one part is honored, every part rejoices with it."* (1 Corinthians 12:25-27)

CULTIVATING A SUPPORTIVE ENVIRONMENT

This verse taught me to share in my son's struggles and triumphs.

To adopt this verse, I took the following practical steps:

When I noticed my son's sad and distracted attitude, I gave him my undivided attention to show him that I was always there for him.

Action Item

How can you show your son that you are there for him when he feels sad?

_____

_____

Achieving a Supportive Environment

An open and non-judgmental environment allows our sons to express their thoughts and emotions. We also have a part to play. Leading by example demonstrates the values we hope to instill. Here are additional practical steps you can take to achieve this.

1. Provide Emotional Support

We must assure them that their feelings are valid. Encouraging a growth mindset helps them embrace challenges and view failures as opportunities for growth.

2. Positive Attention

Showing positive attention instills a message of trust and security. We can show positive attention through smiles, eye contact, gentle physical touch, using kind words that celebrate and lift him, and showing interest in his activities and achievements.

3. Respecting their privacy and empowering decision-making

Both contribute to a healthy, supportive environment. Set clear boundaries and expectations while allowing him autonomy to make his own choices. Staying involved shows your commitment to his well-being and development, creating a foundation for the journey into adulthood.

4. Celebrate Achievements

Celebrate his accomplishments, no matter how small. This can boost his self-esteem and encourage him to open up.

5. Stay Informed

Stay updated on current trends, interests, and challenges teenagers face. This will help you relate to him and initiate relevant discussions.

6. Stay Calm

When conflicts arise, stay calm and composed. Emotional reactions can lead to further misunderstandings.

Impacts of a Non-Supportive Environment

Creating a supportive and nurturing home environment that promotes positive behavior and healthy development for our sons is crucial. Not cultivating a positive atmosphere could unintentionally encourage the development of negative behavior.

When teenage boys are in an unsupportive environment, it can negatively affect their behavior and well-being. One of the consequences is susceptibility to negative peer influence. If they do not receive nurturing and affirmation at home, they may seek validation and acceptance from external sources. This can lead them towards risky behaviors or affiliations.

A lack of support can also erode their self-esteem and self-worth, making them feel like they don't belong or have a purpose. This can cause them to withdraw, become aggressive, or engage in self-destructive activities as they try to deal with feelings of isolation and inadequacy.

Furthermore, an unsupportive environment can hinder their emotional development and communication effectively. They may internalize their feelings without a safe space to express themselves, leading to pent-up frustration or even depression. This can result in difficulties forming healthy relationships and may contribute to challenges in academic or social settings.

The bottom line is we play a pivotal role in our sons' development, especially during their teenage years. Creating a supportive environment can set the stage for their thriving. This bolsters their confidence and encourages healthy emotional expression.

By nurturing their strengths and addressing their challenges positively and affirmatively, a mother empowers her son to take on life's challenges with confidence and determination, paving the way for him to thrive in various aspects of his life.

"Be devoted to one another in love.
Honor one another above yourselves."
Romans 12:10

Prayer

Pray this prayer aloud.

"Dear Heavenly Father, I come before you with a grateful heart, acknowledging that my son is your precious gift. I pray for your guidance and wisdom as I strive to create a loving and supportive environment for him. Help me to be patient and understanding, to listen with an open heart, and to offer words of encouragement that uplift his spirit. Grant me the strength to model compassion, kindness, and forgiveness so that he may learn to extend these virtues to himself and others. Fill our hearts with your presence and grant us the grace to serve you together as a family.

I ask for your hand in shaping our home into a sanctuary of warmth and acceptance. May your love be the cornerstone that binds us, and your wisdom guides us in supporting one another. Help me be a source of strength and support that constantly reminds him of his worthiness and your boundless love for him. Please grant me the humility to admit my shortcomings and the grace to seek forgiveness when needed. Lord, fill our interactions with kindness, understanding, and a deep sense of belonging. May our home reflect your grace, where we grow in faith, wisdom, and mutual support, all to your glory.

In Jesus' name. Amen."

CHAPTER 8

Increasing in the Fruit of the Spirit

"But the fruit of the Spirit is love, joy, peace, longsuffering, gentleness, goodness, faith, meekness, temperance: against such there is no law."
Galatians 5:22-23 KJV

The teachings of the Apostle Paul, found in the book of Galatians, specifically in Chapter 5, verses 22 and 23, unveil a profound revelation of Christ's qualities that blossom within our hearts because of the Holy Spirit.

The fruit of the Spirit represents that spiritual bouquet—a cluster of virtues that reflect the very nature of God and serve as our guide for Christian living.

We will delve deeper into each attribute, uncovering their significance, relevance to our daily lives, and the profound impact they can have on the relationship with our sons.

Before exploring each characteristic, let's first understand why it's called the fruit of the Spirit.

Fruit = *Product of the plant. Results. The effect or consequence of one's work. What you bear.*

Spirit = *The Holy Spirit*

Fruit of the Spirit = *The **by-products** of the nine-character traits (fruit) found in Christ's nature **produced by the Holy Spirit**.*

As mothers, the fruit of the Spirit within us will help guide our challenging journey with our sons. As you contemplate each facet of this spiritual fruit, reflect on your role as a nurturer, protector, and guide to your son.

Connecting your life with Christ is essential to experience your growth. This involves building a deep knowledge, love, and remembrance of Him while striving to imitate His actions.

By doing so, we can fulfill the goal of the law, which is to love both God and our neighbors and live in peace.

Love

Love is the foundation of all the other attributes. It involves selfless, unconditional love for others, as exemplified by God's love for humanity. Allow your love to manifest in your actions. This is how the Bible defines love:

> *"Love is patient, love is kind. It does not envy, it does not boast, it is not proud. It does not dishonor others, it is not self-seeking, it is not easily angered, it keeps no record of wrongs. Love does not delight in evil but rejoices with the*

truth. It always protects, always trusts, always hopes, always perseveres. Love never fails. But where there are prophecies, they will cease; where there are tongues, they will be stilled; where there is knowledge, it will pass away."
(1 Corinthians 13:4-8)

As Mothers: Love is both a feeling and a deliberate, unconditional choice. You express your love through sleepless nights, sacrifices, and affection for your son.

Action Step to Display this Character:

Self-Care: It's crucial to practice self-care. Show love to yourself by setting aside time for your interests, hobbies, and well-being. This sets an example for your son about self-love and balance.

Forgiveness: Display love by forgiving and letting go of his past mistakes or conflicts. Forgiveness allows both of you to move forward without holding onto resentment.

Joy

Joy is a deep and abiding sense of inner happiness and contentment, not dependent on external circumstances. For the joy of the Lord brings forth joy. *"May the God of hope fill you with all joy and peace as you trust in him, so that you may overflow with hope by the power of the Holy Spirit" (Romans 15:13).*

As Mothers: Joy isn't limited to happiness during good times. It can be found in the everyday moments spent with our sons, such as their laughter, milestones, and challenges. Joy reminds us to appreciate these moments and recognize the beauty in the ordinary.

Action Step to Display this Character:

Create a Positive Environment: Foster a positive home environment by focusing on kindness, encouragement, and optimism. When your home is a place of positivity and support, it can create a sense of joy.

Share Laughter: Find moments to share laughter and humor. Watch a funny movie together, share jokes, or reminisce about humorous family stories. Laughter can be a powerful source of joy and bonding.

Peace

Peace is the inner calm and serenity of a harmonious relationship, even in life's challenges. *"Blessed are the peacemakers, for they will be called children of God" (Matthew 5:9).*

As Mothers: Practicing peace every day is essential. I realize our sons are on the path to discovering adulthood. We must guide patiently, even when they push us to the limit. This mindset reminds me that growth is a gradual process, and each moment presents a chance to learn and improve.

Action Step to Display this Character:

Count to Ten: When you feel your patience wearing thin, take a moment to count to ten before responding to a frustrating situation. This brief pause can help you collect your thoughts and react more calmly.

Use "I" Statements: When discussing concerns or conflicts, use "I" statements to express your feelings without blaming or criticizing. For example, say, "I feel worried when..." instead of "You always..."

Longsuffering

It allows you not to enter fear but endure until you reach the end of your struggle. To have patience, face trials and difficulties with a long-suffering and steadfast spirit without becoming easily angered or frustrated. *"Be still before the Lord and wait patiently for him; do not fret when people succeed in their ways, when they carry out their wicked schemes" (Psalm 37:7).*

As Mothers: God's peace guides you through motherhood's chaos and uncertainties. It reminds you to trust in His plan, even when faced with parenting dilemmas and worries. Patience allows you to create a harmonious and secure environment.

Action Step to Display this Character:

Time for Reflection: Encourage time for personal reflection and journaling. This practice allows you and your son to process emotions and thoughts, leading to greater peace of mind.

Express Empathy: Show empathy towards your son's

feelings and experiences. Validate his emotions, even if you don't always agree. Empathy fosters understanding and reduces tension.

Gentleness

Kindness involves showing sympathy and understanding—a compassionate and benevolent attitude toward others characterized by acts of goodwill and empathy. *"Anxiety weighs down the heart, but a kind word cheers it up" (Proverbs 12:25).*

As Mothers: Kindness is at the heart of teaching empathy and compassion. It's about modeling a caring attitude and encouraging them to be considerate and helpful to others. It reminds us to speak to them with gentleness and understanding.

Action Step to Display this Character:

Avoid Harsh Criticism: Be mindful of your words and tone. Avoid hurtful comments. Instead, offer constructive feedback with kindness and encouragement.

Celebrate Achievements: Celebrate your son's achievements, no matter how small they may seem. Kindness involves acknowledging his efforts and accomplishments and expressing pride in his successes.

Goodness

Goodness refers to moral excellence and uprightness, living in a way that reflects God's goodness and righteousness in all aspects of life. True goodness comes from God, who is Holy, Righteous, merciful, and loving. *"In the same way, let your light shine before others, that they may see your good deeds and glorify your Father in heaven"* (Matthew 5:16).

As Mothers: Goodness reminds us to lead by example. It's about living a life of integrity, honesty, and moral uprightness so our sons can learn the values that will guide them.

Action Step to Display this Character:

Self-Reflection: Encourage self-reflection in both you and your son. Periodically assess your actions and choices, aiming to align them with principles of goodness. Share your reflections with him to model the process.

Volunteer Together: Participate in volunteer activities or community service together. This provides an opportunity to show the value of giving back and making a positive impact on the lives of others.

Faith

Faithfulness means being trustworthy and dependable in your commitments to you and your son. *"Have faith in the Lord your God and you will be upheld; have faith in his prophets and you will be successful"* (2 Chronicles 20:20).

As Mothers: Faithfulness is about keeping our promises and being a reliable source of support and guidance. It's about instilling trust and consistency in our relationship.

Action Step to Display this Character:

> **Keep Promises**: Always keep your promises to your son, whether it's a promise to attend his school event or to help with a project. Following through on commitments fosters trust and faithfulness.

> **Prioritize Quality Time**: Allocate quality time for one-on-one interactions. These moments of connection reinforce your faithfulness to your relationship and his well-being.

Meekness

Gentleness is a humble and meek demeanor that shows humility and consideration in our interactions. *"Blessed are the meek, for they will inherit the earth"* (Matthew 5:5).

As Mothers: Gentleness is crucial in our interactions. It reminds us to approach discipline with a loving and tender demeanor, helping them understand the importance of empathy and respect in their relationships.

Action Step to Display this Character:

> **Apologize When Necessary**: If you make a mistake or respond with impatience or harshness, be willing to apologize and make amends. This demonstrates

humility and the importance of gentleness in relationships.

Share Personal Stories: Share personal stories and experiences from your teenage years to let him know you understand his challenges. This vulnerability can strengthen your bond and create a sense of connection.

Temperance

Self-control and restraint over desires, impulses, and actions allow you to make wise choices. *"Now the overseer is to be above reproach, faithful to his wife, temperate, self-controlled, respectable, hospitable, able to teach" (1 Timothy 3:2).*

As Mothers: Self-control teaches us to manage our reactions and emotions. It's about modeling self-discipline and emotional regulation so they can learn these essential life skills.

Action Step to Display this Character:

Healthy Lifestyle Choices: Make healthy lifestyle choices regarding nutrition and exercise. Show your son the importance of self-control in maintaining a balanced and healthy life.

Stay Calm in Crisis: In challenging situations or emergencies, maintain a calm and composed demeanor. Your ability to stay in control during crises teaches your son resilience and self-control.

Which characteristic do you need the Holy Spirit to increase in you? *Love, joy, peace, longsuffering, gentleness, goodness, faith, meekness, temperance.*

Let's ask God to help in that area you identified.

Prayer

Pray this prayer aloud.

"Heavenly Father, I need your strength and guidance in this challenging time. I pray for the fruit of the Spirit to manifest in my life. Fill me with an extra measure of love so he may feel the depth of my care and support even amidst his defiance. May your joy be a beacon of light in our home, reminding us that even in difficult moments, there is hope and happiness to be found. Instill a peace that surpasses all understanding, allowing me to remain calm and steady in the face of turmoil. Give me the wisdom to discern the root of his rebellion and guide me in offering gentle correction and guidance, always with gentleness and respect.

Lord, I ask for an overflow of gentleness and goodness in my interactions with my son. Help me see beyond his rebellious actions and recognize the potential and goodness within him. Fill me with faithfulness that I may remain steadfast in my support for him, even when the path ahead seems uncertain. Grant me the gift of longsuffering, so I may respond to his challenges with measured words and actions rather than reacting in frustration or anger. Finally, I ask for an extra measure of gentleness so that I may approach him with a spirit of tenderness and humility, creating a safe space for him to express himself. May your fruit of the Spirit be in our lives, bringing healing, restoration, and a renewed sense of unity.

In Jesus' name. Amen."

CHAPTER 9

Facing The Man in The Mirror

"For now we see only a reflection as in a mirror;
then we shall see face to face. Now I know in part;
then I shall know fully, even as I am fully known."
1 Corinthians 14:2

Some people may consider it narcissistic when someone often stares at himself in the mirror. However, it is worth noting that looking at your reflection can help uncover hidden truths about yourself. Once you acknowledge and work through these truths, the mirror can become a tool for improving your relationships and emotional strength. That same mirror can also help you stay present with yourself and help you tap into a new inner power.

Think about what a mirror does. Its main job is to reflect what it sees, revealing the reality of what appears in front of it. If you are anything like me, there are times when I often guide the mirror only to observe what I want it to see. I focus only on what I value as my strengths and avoid my weaknesses.

I struggled with my weight for some time, noticing my clothes becoming tighter. To avoid facing reality, I only looked at the upper half of my body. However, during a night out with friends, a selfie revealed my actual weight. That image forced me to look at myself in a full mirror. I cried as it reflected my truth.

That experience taught me a valuable lesson. When we conceal our imperfections, they are still observable to others. It was time to deal with my truth. I began to look at my reflection in the mirror, not to focus on my appearance or to imagine how I looked to others but to acknowledge myself.

When we open ourselves up completely, the mirror can reveal the concealed areas that have altered our self-perception. In my case, I realized that it was time to take control of my weight. Though I wasn't happy with what I saw, I was determined to change my truth until I saw my new reality.

Our sons inwardly value the feedback they receive from others. Instead of relying on the truth revealed by a mirror, they turn to social media, peers, and people they trust. These influences share their perspectives, opinions, and dressed-up lifestyles, which our sons use to guide their mirrors to only what they choose to see in themselves. The mirror reflects only what is captured, leaving the truth hidden away.

Embracing the Observation from the Mirror

"But be transformed by the renewing of your mind."
Romans 12:2

Like a mirror, God reveals our truth, reflecting our actual image of what He sees when looking at us. The book of Genesis tells us, *"So God created mankind in his image, in the image of God he created them; male and female he created them"* (Genesis 1:27). This verse highlights every individual's inherent dignity and worth, emphasizing that we all carry God's imprint, recognizing ourselves and our sons as a reflection of God's image and likeness. This is what God's mirror displays to us.

When we look thoroughly into God's mirror, the qualities reflected are love, compassion, reason, creativity, and a sense of justice, all of which originate from God.

When our sons haven't developed a personal relationship with God, they can easily be enticed to look into the world's mirror. Its reflection only displays superficial measures of success, like physical appearance, material wealth, popularity, and an unrealistic standard of perfection. They are then compelled to fit into this predetermined mold for validation and acceptance.

Their lack of understanding of what it means to be children of God prevents them from embracing their true identity. As their mother, we must reintroduce them to the knowledge of God and how they were created in His image. When they walk into that identity, their negative influencers can no longer have control over how they should act and feel.

So, how do we help them discover this true identity? Teaching them how to look into God's full mirror.

A Re-Introduction to Jesus

Igniting that desire in them will require transforming how they perceive themselves. God reveals that this can only begin with the renewal of their mind (Romans 12:2).

Teaching your son to renew his mind and develop a healthy perspective in the age of social media can be achieved. Before we ask our son to stand in front of God's mirror, we must re-introduce God to him.

One way to make a strong statement about our faith in Jesus is to allow our sons to see how much He means to us. Take a moment to reflect on how you show your love for God in your own home. In my case, I used to rely on the church instead of taking on that responsibility. Attending Sunday services wasn't enough to inspire him to start a relationship with God and stay in front of God's mirror.

I had to learn to become the role model I wanted my son to look up to. Children often learn best by observing their parents. I changed my approach in everything I did at home, on the job, or with my family. I demonstrated who Jesus is in my life. For my son, this soon opened his curiosity to connect more with God.

One fantastic way to re-introduce your son to God is by teaching him what God's Word says about him. Don't worry. I'm not asking you to start having Bible study at home. Wait. In a way, I am. However, it doesn't have to be so formal, but it does have to be in a nurturing, loving, and open environment.

Before you start, pray to God what bible verse you and your son should discuss. Fostering a prayerful atmosphere encourages you both to seek guidance and express gratitude. Next, read the passage together and discuss its meaning. Then, share your firsthand experiences that relate to the learnings. You will discover how the Biblical lessons embody the values and virtues that demonstrate kindness, forgiveness, and empathy in interactions with others.

As you move forward, start incorporating scripture into your daily routine. Here are some helpful tips that you can use to steer a thoughtful conversation to draw them to explore their faith by asking questions that automatically lead them back to God's mirror of truth.

- Ask God for His forgiveness.

  Psalm 24:4 teaches that it is important to start prayer with clean hands and a pure heart. To purify ourselves, we must begin by asking God for forgiveness of all wrongdoings.

  I discovered a unique way to manage this task with my son. We set an empty glass bowl on the table. Then, each of us took a sheet of paper and listed all the things we wanted God to forgive us for. Once done, we folded the page and placed it inside the glass bowl without showing it to each other.

  After reciting a prayer, I took a match and lit the paper,

asking God to take these sins and forgive us. As the paper turned into ashes, this symbolic act reminded my son how God never remembers our sins after we ask for forgiveness.

- Have open and honest conversations.

Foster an environment where your son feels safe and comfortable discussing his thoughts and feelings. Encourage open communication and reassure him that it's okay to express himself.

- Be Patient and Non-Critical.

When he shares his thoughts and feelings, avoid judgment or criticism. Be patient and empathetic, even if you disagree with his perspective. Help your son understand that making mistakes is a natural part of self-awareness and personal growth. Encourage him to learn from his mistakes rather than dwelling on them.

Self-awareness

Self-awareness is crucial because it forms the cornerstone of personal growth, emotional intelligence, and effective decision-making. It involves understanding one's thoughts, emotions, strengths, weaknesses, and motivations. With self-awareness, individuals can navigate their lives with greater authenticity, empathy, and resilience. It enables them to recognize and change unhelpful thought patterns, manage their emotions, build healthier relationships, and make informed choices that align with their values and goals. Self-awareness is the foundation for personal development, enabling individuals to lead more fulfilling and purposeful lives while fostering a deeper understanding of themselves and their world.

Ask Open-Ended Questions:

Engage your son in conversations that encourage self-reflection. Ask open-ended questions like: "How did that make you feel?" or "What were you thinking when that happened?" or "Can you tell me more about what's on your mind?" or "What do you like about yourself?"

Encourage Journaling:

Introduce the concept of journaling to your son. Provide him with a notebook or journal where he can write down his thoughts, feelings, and experiences. Encourage him to share what he writes with you when he is comfortable doing so.

Emotion Recognition:

Help your son recognize and label his emotions. You can use emotion cards or books with expressive faces to aid in understanding and discussing feelings.

After specific experiences or events, engage your son in reflection. Ask questions like, "What did you learn from that?" or "How could you manage a similar situation differently next time?"

Encourage Self-Expression:

Support your son in expressing himself through creative outlets like art, music, or writing. These activities can provide a non-verbal way to explore thoughts and emotions.

Developing self-awareness is an ongoing process. Be consistent in your efforts to encourage self-reflection and self-expression. Celebrate small milestones and progress.

Challenge Negative Thoughts

Negative thoughts can perpetuate self-doubt, anxiety, and low self-esteem, hindering personal growth and well-being. By confronting and questioning these negative narratives, our sons can gain a more accurate perspective on themselves and their circumstances, leading to increased self-confidence and a remarkable ability to cope with life's challenges. Challenging negativity opens the door to self-compassion, healthier relationships, and a more optimistic outlook, facilitating personal growth and greater empowerment.

Identify Negative Thoughts:
Help your son recognize negative thoughts when they occur. Teach him to identify patterns, such as self-criticism, self-doubt, or catastrophic thinking.

Challenge Negative Beliefs:
Guide your son in questioning the validity of negative beliefs. Ask him to consider the evidence for and against these thoughts. Encourage him to explore alternative, more positive interpretations.

Replace Negative Thoughts:
Assist him in substituting negative thoughts with more optimistic and realistic ones. For example, if he thinks, "I'll never be good at this," help him rephrase it as, "I may face challenges, but I can improve with effort."

Affirmations:
Teach your son to use positive affirmations. Together, create a list of affirmations, focusing on his strengths and abilities, and encourage him to repeat them daily.

Limit Negative Influences:
Encourage your son to reduce exposure to sources that perpetuate negativity, such as certain social media accounts or peers who engage in destructive thinking. Help him create a more positive environment.

Surround him with people who will uplift and support him. Limit exposure to individuals or situations that reinforce negative self-perceptions.

Changing his thought patterns takes time and effort. Be patient and supportive throughout the process. Realize that setbacks are a natural part of growth. Using these strategies, a mother can empower her son to challenge negative thoughts effectively and develop a more positive and resilient mindset, enhancing his overall well-being and personal development.

Practice Self-Compassion

Practicing self-compassion is vital because it nurtures a kind and understanding relationship with oneself. It involves treating oneself with the same care and empathy as one would offer a dear friend in times of difficulty or self-doubt. By embracing self-compassion, our sons can counteract self-criticism, reduce stress, and bolster their emotional well-being. It provides a buffer against the harsh judgments and unrealistic expectations they often place on themselves, promoting mental resilience and fostering a sense of self-worth. Self-compassion cultivates a healthier self-image, stronger self-esteem, and the capacity to navigate life's challenges with grace and acceptance, contributing to overall happiness and a more fulfilling life.

Normalize Imperfections:
Emphasize that everyone makes mistakes and experiences setbacks. Normalize imperfections by sharing your own and discussing how they can be growth opportunities.

Use Positive Language:
Encourage your son to use positive and self-compassionate language when talking about himself. Replace self-criticism with affirmations and supportive self-talk.

Empathy Practice:
Encourage empathy towards oneself by asking your son

to consider how he would comfort a friend facing a similar challenge. Prompt him to treat himself with the same compassion he would extend to that friend.

Encourage Self-Care:
Teach your son the importance of self-care, including adequate rest, nutrition, and physical activity. These practices are essential for overall well-being and self-compassion.

Daily Affirmation

Now that your son has completed these steps, one last step remains. Ask him to look in the mirror and do the following.

- Stand in its full view.
- Take a deep breath in and out and have him look at himself.
- Observe everything the mirror is reflecting.
- Then have him tell himself: "I love you just the way you are. You are doing better than you think. I am proud of you!"

This affirmation will become easier to repeat over time.

Remember that changing self-perception takes time and effort. It's a continuous journey of self-discovery and growth. Renewing your mind involves consciously shifting your thought patterns and beliefs to align with a healthier and more positive self-image. Invest the time in his personal development. Continuously learn and acquire new skills. The more he achieves and grows, the more his self-image can transform positively.

Create a safe space through genuine care, active listening, and a non-judgmental approach. This nurturing environment allows God to become a natural part of the relationship, nurture his spiritual growth, and help him navigate life's challenges with a foundation of faith and love.

Prayer

Pray this prayer aloud.

"Gracious God, I humbly come to you with a heart overflowing with love and hope for my beloved son. I pray that you bestow upon him the gift of positive self-perception, allowing him to see himself as the incredible and unique individual that he is. May he find within himself the beauty, talents, and potential that you have lovingly woven into his very being.

Lord, help him understand that he is fearfully and wonderfully made in your image, deserving of love and acceptance, especially from himself. Guide him to replace self-doubt and self-criticism with self-appreciation and self-love. Grant him the clarity to recognize his strengths, the resilience to embrace his weaknesses as opportunities for growth, and the confidence to face life's challenges with unwavering self-belief. May he always walk in the light of your love and know that his self-perception reflects the divine masterpiece you have created. In your boundless grace, empower him to journey through life with a positive and uplifting self-perception, shining brightly as a testament to your love and guidance.

In Jesus' name. Amen."

CHAPTER 10

Understanding The Five Love Languages

"Be devoted to one another in love.
Honor one another above yourselves"
Romans 12:10

M arriage counselor Dr. Gary Chapman developed the "Five Love Languages" concept in his book "The Five Love Languages: How to Express Heartfelt Commitment to Your Mate."[1] Initially, he wrote it for disconnected couples who desired to experience a deeper connection. Today, all use his concept to help them understand how to express and receive love their way.

These love languages serve as a framework for enhancing relationships and improving partner communication. Each person typically has a primary love language, and understanding these languages can lead to more fulfilling and harmonious connections.

As individuals, we all have our way of expressing love, known as our love language. It's essential to take the time to understand your son's love language so that your expressions of love are clearly understood and appreciated. This helps prevent misunderstandings, improves communication, and strengthens your connection by showing love in a way that resonates with him the most.

The "Five Love Languages" are like emotional communication styles. They include *Words of Affirmation*, *Acts of Service*, *Receiving Gifts*, *Quality Time*, and *Physical Touch*.

Identifying your primary love language and that of your son allows you to tailor your expressions of love to suit each other's preferences better, making a more harmonious relationship.

WHAT ARE THE FIVE LOVE LANGUAGES

Words of Affirmation

Meaning: To this person, unsolicited compliments and hearing the reason behind your actions make them feel loved. They thrive on hearing encouraging words that build them up.

If this is your love language: Express love through kind words, compliments, and verbal affirmations. Actions don't speak louder than words. Use words to affirm them. Pay attention to the thoughts behind your words and how you vocalize them.

Suggestions: Simple statements like "I love you" or "You mean the world to me." Hand-written notes, spontaneous texts, and meaningful, specific compliments.

What Makes Them Feel Unloved: Negative words.

Acts of Service

Meaning: This person believes that actions speak louder than words and prefers non-verbal displays of love. Serving out of love, not obligation, allows him to feel loved.

If this is your love language: Do things to show your love and care. Do something that relieves their burden to make life easier or more enjoyable.

Suggestions: Helping him with homework. Saying, "Let me do that with you."

What Makes Them Feel Unloved: Broken commitments. Making him do more work. These actions suggest their feelings do not matter.

Receiving Gifts

Meaning: To this person, a thought-out gift or gesture shows they are known and cared for. They thrive on the thoughtfulness and the effort behind the gift. Gifts to them are heartfelt symbols of love.

If this is your love language: Give and receive thoughtful tokens of affection. Do not mistake this for materialism. These gifts do not have to be extravagant. The gesture is far more critical than the actual gift itself. It is the sentiment and thought behind the gift that matters.

Suggestions: Do not break the bank. Start with something small. But it must be a tangible gift demonstrating you "get" him and know what he likes.

What Makes Them Feel Unloved: The absence of everyday gestures. A missed birthday. Acting hasty, thoughtless. All would be disastrous.

Quality Time

Meaning: To this person, giving your undivided attention and being fully present makes them feel unique and loved.

If this is your love language: Give your undivided attention. Being there and actively listening to them.

Suggestions: Engaging in meaningful conversations, watching TV, or playing video games together. Share a hobby.

What Makes Them Feel Unloved: Distractions. Postponing activities. Failure to listen. All are incredibly hurtful.

Physical Touch

Meaning: Nothing speaks more deeply to this person than appropriate physical touch. They are sometimes very touchy.

If this is your love language: Give physical expressions of love. Your physical presence and accessibility are crucial. Appropriate and timely touches communicate warmth, safety, and love.

Suggestions: Good morning hugs, a kiss on the cheek, holding hands, cuddling, and other forms of physical affection. Always look for opportunities to connect physically.

What Makes Them Feel Unloved: Neglect or physical abuse can be unforgettable and destructive.

. . .

Identify Your Love Language

While it's important to know your son's love language, equally important is understanding yours.

STEP 1: *Observation*

Chapman suggests that to identify someone's love language, paying attention to how they show love to others is essential.

People show love in the way that they want to receive it. Pay attention to cues and signals from your son about what makes him feel loved. Sometimes, it is not just about the explicit use of love language but also about recognizing subtle expressions of love.

STEP 2: *What Is Your Love Language*

Select, or copy and paste, this link to take the Five Love Languages test:

https://5lovelanguages.com/quizzes/love-language

Take this 30-question quiz to help you determine your primary love language. Communicate your results with each other to help them better understand what makes you feel appreciated.

Discovering your son's love language (and vice versa) can lead to a more robust, happier relationship, even if your primary languages differ.

. . .

STEP 3: *Communication*

Have open and honest conversations about your primary love language with each other. Ask your son how he feels loved. Share your preferences as well.

STEP 4: *Flexibility*

While you can focus on each other's primary love languages, it's also helpful to be flexible and adaptable to meet each other's needs, especially in times of change or stress.

STEP 5: *Consistency*

Consistently practicing these love languages helps build a solid and lasting bond between a mother and her son.

Practice Your Love Language

We all express and receive love differently. Learning and understanding those differences can have a meaningful impact on your relationship. According to Chapman, this is one of the simplest ways to improve your relationship.

Applying the concept of Five Love Languages can deepen your relationship and create a more loving and supportive connection.

Prayer

Pray this prayer aloud with me.

"Lord, I come before you with a heart full of gratitude for the gift of love and the unique ways we can express it. Thank you for creating us with diverse love languages, each reflecting a beautiful aspect of your love. I lift my family to you and ask for your guidance in understanding and speaking each other's love languages.

Help me express words of affirmation to my son and speak kindness and encouragement into his life. Let my words reflect your love and build him up in faith and confidence. Guide me in acts of service, Lord, that I may serve my family with a willing heart, demonstrating my love through actions that ease their burdens and bring them joy.

Teach me to give and receive gifts thoughtfully, not for material gain but as symbols of our love and appreciation for one another. Lead us to spend quality time together, Lord, where we can bond, share, and create cherished memories. Help me prioritize these moments in my busy life.

May we express physical affection, offering hugs, kisses, and warm embraces, understanding that these gestures tangibly convey love.

Let our love for one another reflect your perfect love for us. May we seek to understand and meet each other's needs in the love languages that resonate with our hearts. In doing so, may our family grow stronger and closer, bound together by your love. We offer this prayer in the name of Jesus Christ, our ultimate example of love. Amen."

CHAPTER 11

Opening Lines of Communication

"The tongue has the power of life and death."
Proverbs 18:21

O ur words have power. Power to lift someone or tear them down. How you use that power is up to you. Words can brighten a day with a compliment or darken it with a snide remark.

The power of our words means that we are responsible for recognizing that our sons have feelings, worries, and expectations often hidden when communicating. We should be generous, giving them the benefit of the doubt. Assume the best and not the worst.

When communicating with your son, take a moment to pause and reflect before reacting. It's important not to let your emotions guide your words and actions. How you respond when he's not at his best can significantly impact the relationship. He will leave the discussion feeling heard and acknowledged, reinforcing his self-worth and importance.

Open Communication Builds Healthy Self-Esteem

Building his self-esteem through open communication is a robust foundation for fostering healthy emotional development. Open and honest dialogue provides a safe space for our sons to express their thoughts, feelings, and concerns, knowing they are heard and valued. Several critical aspects contribute to building and maintaining robust self-esteem.

Benefits of Open Communication:

Open communication allows you to give helpful feedback and guidance. You can gently correct any misunderstandings or negative self-image he may have and provide a more accurate view of his abilities and potential. When he faces challenges or makes mistakes, approach the situation supportively and help him understand that making errors is a normal part of learning and growth and does not determine his value.

Having open communication can create a feeling of trust and safety. He can develop a secure attachment if he feels comfortable confiding in his mother without worrying about being judged or rejected. This secure attachment is essential in forming healthy relationships and helps him believe he is worthy of love and acceptance.

In addition, open communication can help you teach essential life skills like regulating his emotions, solving problems, and handling conflicts. These skills will give him the confidence to tackle life's obstacles and learn to manage different situations.

Lastly, open communication allows you to discuss the importance of self-care, boundaries, and self-acceptance instills self-compassion and positive self-perception.

Practical Steps

Here are some practical steps to take to achieve open communication:

Before You Start

Create the Environment

Decide in advance on a mutually comfortable location at home or elsewhere that invites open discussion. For me, I asked my son to go to the park. This was a space where we both felt safe to express our feelings. No matter where you choose, make sure it's a relaxing space free from distractions.

Start With Forgiveness

Extending forgiveness lays the foundation for communication. It creates a safe and nurturing environment where both parties can express themselves without fear of judgment or resentment.

Forgiveness also sets a powerful example to teach him the value of empathy, compassion, and taking responsibility for his actions. You can move forward from past conflicts and build a stronger, more trusting relationship. Starting with forgiveness is an act of strength that lays the groundwork for a more harmonious and fulfilling relationship.

Invite God into the Conversation

Before starting the conversation, I recommend praying and inviting God to join you. This will enable Him to steer the discussion and unveil truths that might otherwise remain concealed. His involvement allows you to approach the conversation lovingly, promoting positive communication and facilitating healing.

Respect Privacy

Maintaining a balance between open communication and respecting his privacy is crucial. If he feels uneasy about discussing something, reassure him you're there to listen whenever he's ready. Forcing him to talk may cause him to withdraw further, so it's vital to prioritize maintaining a safe space and avoid pressuring him to share everything all at once. So, give him space when needed.

Be Patient

Patience is a cornerstone of effective communication. Firstly, it acknowledges that understanding and growth take time. Remember, adolescence is a crucial development phase. Your patience allows him the space to navigate this journey at his own pace.

Having patience demonstrates respect for his unique perspective and individuality. It shows you value his thoughts and feelings, fostering a sense of self-worth and confidence.

Patience allows you to create a non-threatening atmosphere where he feels comfortable expressing himself without fear of immediate criticism or reprimand. This, in turn, encourages honesty and transparency in conversation.

By demonstrating patience, you are setting a positive example. Teaching him the value of patience in relationships and navigating challenging conversations with grace and understanding will help him grow into a compassionate and empathetic individual. When confronted with challenges or disagreements, a patient mother is more capable of handling conflicts with empathy and finding a resolution instead of making matters worse.

DURING THE CONVERSATION

Initiate Meaningful Conversations

Regularly conversing with your son is a beautiful way to understand his perspective and concerns. It is best to pick relaxed moments when both of you are receptive and attentive to each other. This will create an environment where your son feels comfortable sharing his thoughts and feelings, building trust and empathy in your relationship.

Practice Active Listening

> *"Being listened to is so close to being LOVED that most people cannot tell the difference."*
> *David Augsberger*

As a parent, it is crucial to make a conscious effort to listen to his thoughts and feelings truly. We can establish a deeper trust and understanding in our relationship by actively engaging in conversation and acknowledging his emotions.

Validating his perspectives can also demonstrate your respect for his individuality and help him feel heard and valued. Connecting with your son on this level can create a stronger bond and foster a healthy, positive dynamic between you both.

Luke 6:45 tells us, "For the mouth speaks what the heart is full of." Listening to your son openly and without judgment allows you to understand better what's in his heart. This will bring you closer and improve your communication. So, when he speaks, be nonjudgmental and avoid reacting negatively, even if you disagree with his viewpoint.

Practice active listening to show that his words matter.

- Give your full attention when he talks.
- Maintain eye contact.
- Nod and offer encouraging verbal cues like "I understand" or "Tell me more."

Set aside regular time to listen to your son. Encourage him to share his thoughts, feelings, and experiences without interruption. This will help you gain insight into his perspective.

Show Vulnerability and Empathy

You are sharing your experiences and emotions. This will help bridge the generation gap and create a sense of connection. Talk about your teenage years, including the challenges you faced and the lessons you learned. Showing vulnerability communicates that it's okay to struggle and make mistakes while emphasizing the importance of learning and personal growth.

Ask Open-Ended Questions

Instead of asking yes-or-no questions, ask open-ended ones that encourage him to express himself more fully. For example, instead of asking, "Did you have a good day?" ask, "Tell me about your day. What was the best part?"

Respectful Communication by Speaking Life

"Know this, my beloved brothers: let every person be quick to hear, slow to speak, slow to anger."
James 1:19

What we say and how we say it carries impact. God gives us daily opportunities to use our words to make a positive impression on those around us.

It is essential to show the same consideration and mindfulness when talking with your son. This fosters positive relationships and meaningful interactions.

Remember to approach the conversation with an open mind and a willingness to listen and understand his perspective. Doing so can create a safe and welcoming environment for all parties involved. Because what you say and do and how you respond to others can make all the difference.

The power in your words brings forth life in others.

- Speak goodness to those seeking to hear it.
- Touch his life by being kind and courageous when speaking.
- Be gentle with your words because he wants to hear kindness from you. This will save him from himself.

When your son exhibits rebellious behavior, responding respectfully and patiently is essential. Instead of getting frustrated or angry, try to communicate calmly. Take a deep breath and address the situation without raising your voice. This approach values open and respectful dialogue, which can encourage your son to respond kindly.

AFTER THE CONVERSATION

Self-Reflection

Ask yourself, what did I learn?

After engaging in open communication with your son, it is crucial to take the time for self-reflection on the conversation for several reasons. Firstly, self-reflection allows you to process the information and emotions shared. This helps you gain deeper insights into your son's thoughts, feelings, and perspectives, which can lead to a better understanding of his needs and concerns.

Self-reflection enables you to assess your reactions and behaviors during the conversation. It helps you identify any biases, assumptions, or triggers that might have influenced your responses. This self-awareness is vital for personal growth and improving your communication skills.

Moreover, self-reflection fosters empathy. By considering your son's viewpoint and the impact of your words and actions, you can develop a more empathetic and compassionate approach to future conversations. You can identify areas of agreement, disagreement, and potential solutions. This self-assessment helps you better prepare for future discussions and work towards finding common ground and resolution where needed.

Seek Advice

Establishing trust is crucial when listening to your son. He may bring up topics or questions you don't have all the answers to. There's no "right" way to respond, as some questions may be more challenging than others. It's perfectly acceptable to acknowledge if you feel uneasy or uncertain about how to answer. That's when you suggest you may need to seek advice from others.

It is okay to seek advice after trying this approach, and you still don't see a resolution within the relationship. Here are some options.

- **Trusted Friends or Family Members**: Those members who have experience in parenting or have faced similar challenges can provide valuable insights and emotional support.
- **Parenting Groups or Forums**: Online or in-person parenting groups offer a platform to connect with other parents facing similar situations. They can provide advice, share experiences, and offer practical tips.
- **Mental Health Professionals**: Therapists, counselors, or psychologists with expertise in family dynamics and communication can offer professional guidance and tools to navigate challenges.
- **Parenting Coaches**: Certified parenting coaches provide guidance and strategies for effective family communication and conflict resolution.
- **School Counselors or Teachers**: If the communication challenges involve school-related

issues, seeking input from teachers or his school's counselors can be beneficial.

- **Support Groups for Parents of Teens or Adolescents**: These specialized groups focus on the unique challenges of parenting teenagers and can offer specific advice and support tailored to this age group.
- **Online Forums and Communities**: Virtual platforms like online forums, social media groups, and parenting websites provide spaces to seek advice and share experiences with a vast community of parents.
- **Professional Mediators or Counselors**: In cases of significant conflict or strained relationships, seeking the help of a professional mediator or family counselor can provide a neutral space for constructive dialogue.

Remember, seeking advice is a sign of strength and a willingness to grow as a parent. It's essential to choose sources that align with your values and parenting philosophy and always trust your parental instincts.

Open communication is the cornerstone of a nurturing and supportive environment where our son can develop and maintain healthy self-esteem. It offers a platform for emotional support, guidance, trust, and skill-building that empowers him to face life's challenges with confidence and a strong sense of self-worth.

Prayer

Pray this prayer aloud.

"Dear Heavenly Father, I come before you with a humble heart, seeking your guidance and wisdom in nurturing a deeper, more open communication with my precious son. Lord, grant me the strength to be patient, listen with an open heart, and set aside my preconceptions. Help me to see through his eyes and understand his unique perspective. Grant me the grace to offer forgiveness freely, knowing that through this act of love, we can build a foundation of trust. Lord, fill our conversations with your light so we may speak and hear with kindness and empathy. May our words be a source of comfort, encouragement, and support, fostering a stronger bond with each passing day.

Lord, I ask for your divine intervention in those moments of challenge and disagreement. Grant me the wisdom to choose my words carefully and the courage to speak the truth with love. Help me create a safe space where he feels valued and heard and knows his thoughts and feelings are cherished. Lord, bless our relationship with abundant understanding and guide us on this journey of growth and connection. In your loving arms, I place my hopes and prayers for a communication that is honest, open, and filled with the warmth of your eternal love.

In Jesus' name. Amen."

CHAPTER 12

Building Unity

"How good and pleasant it is when God's people **live together in unity!** *It is like precious oil poured on the head, running down on the beard, running down on Aaron's beard, down on the collar of his robe. It is as if the* **dew of Hermon** *were falling on Mount Zion. For there the Lord bestows his blessing, even life forevermore."*
Psalm 133:1-3 [emphasis mine]

To understand the importance of unity, let's first dig deeper into this verse's meaning. The author compares living in unity to that of oil running down the body or the dew of Hermon. Both comparisons are significant.

Aaron, the brother of Moses, whom God chose to become the High Priest to serve Him. Before he could start, Aaron had to set himself apart from all the others and become holy by anointing him by pouring sacred oil over him. This oil would consecrate him and everything he touched (Exodus 30:29-30).

God deemed this oil as sacred and prohibited the Israelites from replicating its formula for personal use, under penalty of being excluded from the community.

So, on the first day of Aaron's Priest ordination, Moses poured the anointing oil onto Aaron's head (Leviticus 8:12), and that oil ran down to the edge of his garments.

Mt Hermon is the highest mountain in Syria, with an elevation of almost 10,000 feet. It was known as the "snowy mountain," the "gray-haired mountain," and the "mountain of snow." It's famous for its heavy dew. Palestine had no rainfall from May or June to September, so the Mediterranean summer climate found relief through the dew as a supplement to rain.

Now, if we revisit the verse – *Living in Unity Is*:

> *It is like the precious oil upon the head, Running down on the beard,*
> *The beard of Aaron, Running down on the edge of his garments.*
> *It is like the dew of Hermon, Descending upon the mountains of Zion.*

Unity represents the harmony that brings blessings to families. The oil flowing down Aaron's garment signifies the depth of Christ's love. His love, acting as a soothing and healing ointment, brings joy to one's heart and creates a sense of peace and contentment.

Additionally, the dew symbolizes the abundance of God's blessings that soften and moisten our hearts, just as the evening dew refreshes the earth.

When a family dwells in unity, they are blessed with peace, health, and joy. So, how can you establish unity in your home?

Bear with each other and forgive one another if any of you has a grievance against someone. Forgive as the Lord forgave you. And over all these virtues put on love, which binds them all together in perfect unity.
—Colossians 3:13-14

Unity is being an agreement with one another. We cannot live in unity without friction and division in the home. The Bible shares several examples of the benefits of staying in unity.

- **Matthew 18:19:** "Again, truly I tell you that if two of you on earth agree about anything they ask for, it will be done for them."
- **Matthew 18:20:** "For where two or three gather in my name, there am I with them."
- **Deuteronomy 32:30:** "How can one man chase a thousand, or two put ten thousand to flight."

The power of agreement is one of the most powerful tools God has given us to use when raising our sons. When two people are united, achieving anything becomes possible.

Amos 3:3 tells us, "Do two walk together unless they have agreed to do so? Agreements align us with good which brings God's love into our lives. That is His secret to our success – Being in unity.

Creating Unity Through Forgiveness

Forgiveness is a powerful tool that brings healing and restoration. When we forgive our sons for their actions, it opens the door to reconciliation and growth. It's not about condoning wrongdoing but about releasing the weight of resentment and anger that can poison the relationship.

Forgiveness allows us to move forward, free from past burdens, creating a space for love, understanding, and grace to flourish. It's an act of strength that paves the way for a renewed and deeper connection, ultimately contributing to the well-being and growth of both individuals.

Here are three practical tips you can consider when forgiving your son.

1) Acknowledge and Validate Feelings: It is essential to acknowledge and validate your feelings, including any hurt, anger, or disappointment you may be experiencing regarding your son. Recognizing and allowing yourself to feel these emotions is the first step toward forgiveness. This self-reflection process can help clarify why forgiveness is essential and what it means for your relationship with your son.

2) Communicate Openly and Honestly: Engage in an open and honest conversation with your son about the actions that caused your hurt. Conduct the dialogue with respect and a genuine desire for understanding. By expressing your feelings and listening to his perspective, you can gain insight into his motivations and intentions, which can be instrumental in the forgiveness process.

3) Focus on the Positive Qualities: Reflecting on your son's positive qualities and remembering moments of love, kindness,

and joy can be a powerful way to shift focus away from hurtful actions. This can help in seeing the bigger picture and nurturing a sense of compassion.

Creating Unity Through Your Actions

You can cultivate an environment of unity that strengthens familial bonds and equip your son with skills and values to navigate life's challenges with love and mutual respect. Be the example of a peacemaker by practicing walking in harmony.

The Disciple-Making Parent published an article titled "Fighting for Unity: 12 Practices that Lead to Family (and Church) Harmony."[1] The report provides steps to promote togetherness.

1. **Pray for unity.** Like Jesus, let's ask the Father to establish unity with our son.
2. **Forbear small matters**. Bearing with or forbearing means overlooking trivial things that will not change. Faultfinding is a natural thing to do. Instead, replace it with thankfulness.
3. **Get the log out of your eye first**. Are you demanding perfection from him? Don't constantly point out the negative in his life and miss your own.
4. **Move toward hard conversations with pleasant words**. The purpose is not to win the disagreement but to win your son back. Mt 18:15 tells us, "If your brother sins against you, go to him." Do not go to other people. Do not let it simmer. Do not avoid conflict. If it is severe enough that you cannot overlook it, then you must work to resolve the matter.

Creating Unity In Your Home

> *"By **wisdom** a house is built,*
> *and through **understanding** it is established;*
> *through **knowledge** its rooms are filled*
> *with rare and beautiful treasures."*
> *Proverbs 24:3-4 [emphasis mine]*

This verse emphasizes the importance of **wisdom**, **understanding**, and **knowledge** in building a home of unity. When these qualities are present, the result is a home filled with valuable and intangible treasures of love, harmony, and a sense of well-being within the family.

Your home can be a place of unity that contributes to a positive and nurturing environment where family members can thrive and find joy.

So, how can we use these crucial attributes in building unity in our home?

Wisdom

Admit it, our wisdom wasn't successful in creating unity with our sons. We must turn to Jesus, asking for His wisdom to help. How?

Study the Scriptures related to God and unity. They will provide valuable insights and guidance on what you can do. Luke 10:5 resonated with me deeply. Upon entering someone's house, the disciples would say, "Peace to this house." Inspired by this, I began speaking these words whenever I entered my home.

Over time, I noticed a positive shift in the atmosphere, and my house felt more welcoming.

Learn from Mistakes by embracing failures as opportunities for growth and learning. During this process, know that you will not always get it right. Recognize that wisdom is a journey, and no one has all the answers. Keep at it. Be open to learning from others and acknowledge when you don't know something. Finally, analyze what went wrong and apply the lessons learned to future situations.

Trust in God's Guidance by seeking Him through prayer and meditation. Trust that He will provide wisdom and discernment in times of uncertainty.

Understanding

To first understand how to create unity in the home, you must discern its current environment. Is your house filled with love and joy or sadness and pain? Whatever the environment, with understanding, it can become a pleasant place to dwell.

Awareness of the overall atmosphere, dynamics, and emotional well-being of family members is essential to understanding the environment at home. Here are some practical ways to achieve this.

Observation: Observe your son's interactions, body language, and expressions. Pay attention to subtle cues indicating their emotional states and overall well-being. When family members share their thoughts or concerns, listen attentively. Avoid interrupting or imposing your own opinions. Instead, validate their feelings and show empathy.

Pay Attention to Changes: Be alert to any significant changes in your son's behavior, mood, or routines. These changes can provide valuable clues about the overall environment in the home.

Reflect on Your Behavior: Consider how your actions, attitudes, and words contribute to the environment. Be mindful of the impact you have on your family members.

Trust Your Intuition: Sometimes, a mother's intuition can provide valuable insights into the home environment. Trust your instincts and be open to adjusting as needed.

Knowledge

To understand what you learned is knowledge. By combining wisdom and understanding, you can use your knowledge to achieve unity.

Knowing is power. Let's see how that power creates unity in your home.

Lead by Example: Model the behavior and values you wish to instill in your son. Demonstrate integrity, honesty, and responsibility to set a positive standard for everyone.

Prioritize Love and Kindness: This is your central

focus when interacting with your son. Show genuine affection, empathy, and compassion to create a warm and supportive atmosphere.

Embrace Flexibility: Be open to new ideas and approaches. Be willing to adapt to changing circumstances. Flexibility promotes creativity and problem-solving within the family.

Prayer

Pray this prayer aloud.

"Heavenly Father, I humbly seek your wisdom, knowledge, and understanding to foster unity in my home. Please grant me the insight to recognize and honor my son's unique needs and the grace to communicate with empathy and kindness. Guide me in making decisions that promote mutual respect and harmony.

Lord, bless me with the knowledge to create a loving and supportive environment. Help me understand my son's heart and aspirations and grant us open and honest communication. May our home be filled with your presence, a sanctuary of peace, love, and understanding. I trust that with your guidance, our family will thrive in unity.

In Jesus' name. Amen."

Conclusion: Starting Your New Life

"There is a time for everything,
and a season for every activity under the heavens:
a time to be born and a time to die,
a time to plant and a time to uproot."
Ecclesiastes 3:1-2

Writing this book was not an easy task. Mentally, I had to prepare myself with God's help when He instructed me to write again after my first book, **Prayer Works! Provoking God to Move**.

My experience with God has taught me that when He wants to minister to His people, He first ministers to you. The area He deals with can be painful at first, but as you continue to move forward, the healing comes.

I've learned that God's healing comes in stages.

First, He mentions a painful area of your life and provides you enough room to experience your emotions.

Next, He exposes the root cause of that painful area and explains why you had to go through it.

Then, He heals you in that area, so the issue no longer troubles you.

Finally, He asks you to share your story to provide hope and inspiration to others facing similar issues.

God's wisdom is great; He knows when we can take those final steps towards wholeness. In my case, the healing was instant, but it took me ten years to become whole.

Writing this book taught me that our actions stem from our thoughts shaped by our past experiences. Our minds gather and store memories from our life's journey, influencing our thoughts and behaviors.

However, regardless of our memories, God's love can still enter our lives and allow us to thrive. To achieve this, we must allow Him to renew our minds and wash away any hurt or harm we experience.

As we conclude this journey of empowering our sons, let us reflect on the remarkable growth and transformation we have witnessed. Through each chapter, we have explored the profound impact you can have on his self-esteem, from the foundational elements to the practical strategies that guide him toward confidence and resilience.

Remember, this journey is not a destination but a continuous, lifelong commitment. Our role as mothers extends far beyond the final page of this book. It is a journey marked by love, patience, and unwavering support. Along the way, there will be moments of triumph and challenge. Through it all, may we find solace in the knowledge that we are shaping young men who are strong, capable, and have boundless potential.

As we stand on the precipice of their future, let us do so with hearts full of hope and gratitude. Our sons embark on their uniquely own path, carrying the lessons and love we have imparted. As they spread their wings, may they soar with confidence, knowing a mother's enduring love supports them.

Speaking of support, I'd love to support you in prayer. You can also find me LIVE on Facebook weekly in my Facebook Group, "Praying in My Car." Here, I share great biblical principles to empower you and refuel your soul.

Just visit: Facebook.com/groups/OktoPray

Thank you for joining me on this transformative journey. May you find joy and purpose in empowering the next generation of extraordinary individuals.

I pray that you allow God to guide you until you are ready to help someone else receive their healing journey.

With heartfelt blessings,

Val Mitchell

Were You Blessed?

Thank you for following along on my journey. In writing this book, I aim to build a strong connection with you and give you hope that your son can be saved.

I hope I've provided practical tools you and your son can use to build your relationship.

I put my heart and soul into strengthening my relationship with my son. As a result, I learned some valuable lessons that I pray you can benefit from after reading my story.

After God asked me to share my journey, I poured hundreds of hours into writing this book, edited it six times (with my son proofing every version), and many other behind-the-scenes stuff. It's been a massive project to complete.

This book means a lot to me as it's my way to help, inspire, and hopefully rebuild bonds between mothers and sons.

COULD YOU PLEASE DO ME A SMALL FAVOR?

Can you take a moment to share your heartfelt thoughts about my book on Amazon?

Your review will help someone who hasn't read my book know why they should take their time to read it.

I love getting honest feedback and will read every review, including yours. Reviews make a HUGE difference to authors. Writing a review is the very best way to help me out.

Please go to post your review:
Review.WorriedAboutMySon.com

Acknowledgments

When God desires to communicate a message to the world, He selects a willing messenger to deliver His Word. I am still unsure why He chose me for this great task, but I feel incredibly grateful for the opportunity.

When I agreed to His plan, I was unsure how to accomplish it. I felt like Moses when God tasked him with delivering the Hebrews from Pharaoh's slavery. However, like Moses, God placed me around the right people to ensure the success of this book.

My journey started with the guidance of my mentor and pastor, Dr. Jerome Glenn, at New Life Church Southeast in Chicago, Illinois. After finishing his latest book, *Take A Seat. Discover Your Significance*, he prayed for me to find the gift of writing within me. He also shared his writing process, which he accomplished in only four weeks. His advice was to prioritize writing daily and devote uninterrupted time to it. He emphasized the importance of focusing on writing first and only then reviewing the work. I took his advice seriously. I set my alarm for 4:30 a.m. every day and went to work.

Next, God ordered my steps to the feet of my second mentor, Donna Partow, a million-copy bestselling author of ***Becoming*** *the **Woman God Wants Me to Be***. Her "Jersey style" approach, as she calls it, forced me to stay disciplined in meeting my deadlines.

Finally, God placed two dear therapists in my path to ensure I understood how our mental affects our behavior. All these factors came together to make this book a reality.

I want to acknowledge these exceptional leaders who played a pivotal role in bringing my book to life. Each recognized the potential within me and helped me birth this creation. This book would not have come to fruition without their guidance and support. It's worth noting that this book was completed in the ninth month, often associated with birthing in Christian beliefs.

When God gives you a task to complete, it could be starting a business, pursuing a degree, or authoring a book, when you give Him your Yes. He will ensure that you are well-equipped to finish the task.

Thank you, God, for entrusting me with delivering a message to mothers crying out to find a common ground with their sons.

About the Author

Val Mitchell is a God-focused transformational speaker, teacher, and coach whose mission is healing women's souls by equipping them with tools to help them achieve their divine purpose. Val is thoroughly convinced of the power of prayer. With God as the head of her life, she has seen firsthand the effects of a daily prayer life. Val has a heart to serve, whether going on missionary trips, empowering moms living in shelters, praying for others, or assisting in several ministries within her local church.

Val earned a bachelor's degree from Tennessee State University, a master's degree from Central Michigan University, and a Life Coach certification. Val currently resides in Detroit, MI. She is a proud mother of three terrific young men.

These days, Val hosts a weekly Facebook live ministry called "Praying in My Car" with hashtag #OK2Pray. She teaches biblical principles from the comfort of her vehicle. Val received a prophetic word: she was a light that would draw souls to God. Since that word, God has allowed her to do just that. Val's motto is found in Romans 12:2, *"Do not conform to the pattern of this world but be transformed by the renewing of your mind."*

 facebook.com/OK2Pray

More Books by Val Mitchell

Prayer Works: Provoking God to Respond Paperback

Like many Christians, Val Mitchell felt that prayer didn't work. Then she discovered the true purpose of prayer. She took a unique approach...and instantly, everything changed for her. When you discover the truth, everything will change for you, too.

In Prayer Works, Val reveals:

- Why prayer always works
- How to pray the right way

How to never be disappointed by unanswered prayers again: Get free from the distractions that hinder prayer.

Plus, there are great examples of prayers from the Bible to help you grow in praying scripture.

Whether your motivation is praying for your children while they are still young or for adult children, this book will provide fresh encouragement. You can become part of the growing army of praying women God is raising. Prayer Works will show you exactly how.

The Prayers of the Righteous: 10 Prayers to Get God Moving

The question of whether Jesus hears my prayers engulfs me countless times.

Prayer is used to redirect God's attention to you. Many of us are unaware of our special relationship with Jesus. His ultimate sacrifice on the cross opened the door to approach God with anything.

Righteousness is quite simple. When you allow God to lead, He takes you to a victorious destination. This path followed leads the way to righteousness. Regardless of your past, you have a place in God's heart.

In Prayers of the Righteous, I reveal why:

- God calls you righteous.
- You shouldn't stop seeking God for answers
- Prayer works

The book also contains excellent examples to help you grow in prayer.

Whether your motivation is praying over your children, family, or your career, this book will provide fresh encouragement. You, too, can be counted as having a Righteous Prayer Life.

The book also includes a link to download a free guide to 7 Step Guide to Why We Pray.

Notes

INTRODUCTION

1. [1] *Suicide rate highest among teens and young adults.* (n.d.). Retrieved September 15, 2023, from https://www.uclahealth.org/news/suicide-rate-highest-among-teens-and-young-adults
2. [2] *Suicide Data and Statistics | Suicide | CDC.* (2023, August 15). https://www.cdc.gov/suicide/suicide-data-statistics.html
3. Gaylor, E. M. (2023). Suicidal Thoughts and Behaviors Among High School Students—Youth Risk Behavior Survey, United States, 2021. *MMWR Supplements, 72.* https://doi.org/10.15585/mmwr.su7201a6
4. *Ohio State football player Harry Miller retires, citing mental health concerns.* (n.d.). Retrieved September 15, 2023, from https://www.nbcnews.com/news/us-news/ohio-state-football-player-retires-game-citing-mental-health-concerns-rcna19661

3. ISHMAEL'S STORY

1. *Galatians 4:21–31.* ESV Bible. (n.d.). https://www.esv.org/verses/Galatians%204%3A21-31/

4. THE MINDSET OF AN ADOLESCENT

1. *What Are Cognitive Processes? Definition, Types and Uses | Indeed.com.* (n.d.). Retrieved September 15, 2023, from https://www.indeed.com/career-advice/career-development/cognitive-processes
2. Bond, L., Butler, H., Thomas, L., Carlin, J., Glover, S., Bowes, G., & Patton, G. (2007). Social and school connectedness in early secondary school as predictors of late teenage substance use, mental health, and academic outcomes. *Journal of adolescent health, 40*(4), 357-e9.

5. A HEALTHY MINDSET

1. Advanced Solutions International, Inc. (n.d.). *Do you have a comprehensive picture of Your Students' Health?* NCHA Home. https://www.acha.org/NCHA/NCHA_Home

10. UNDERSTANDING THE FIVE LOVE LANGUAGES

1. *Discover your love language® - the 5 love languages®.* Discover Your Love Language® - The 5 Love Languages®. (n.d.). https://5lovelanguages.com/

12. BUILDING UNITY

1. *Fighting for Unity: 12 Practices that Lead to Family (and Church) Harmony—The Disciple-Making Parent.* (n.d.). Retrieved September 15, 2023, from https://www.thedisciplemakingparent.com/fighting-for-unity-12-practices-that-lead-to-family-and-church-harmony/